SECRETS

of Our

Hidden Controllers

Revealed

By:

Larry Flinchpaugh
5500 Cape Court
St. Joseph, Mo. 64503

Email: lflinch@stjoelive.com

www.larryflinchpaugh.com

ISBN 978-0-615-28058-5

First Printing February 12, 2009
Second printing November 1, 2009
Third Printing March 16, 2012
Fourth Printing April 28, 2013

-Forward-

After retirement, for the first time in my life, I found the time and the energy to pursue the role of a 'political activist'! In so doing, I discovered that many of our opinions regarding politics, our educational system, and even our religious organizations **have become** so distorted that we often fail to make the proper decisions in electing those officials who will save our country from deteriorating into a third world status.

This book stresses that every one of us needs to get involved in electing those representatives who will support a small Federal Government, (1) who abides by the Constitution, (2) who believes in sound monetary policies including abolishing the private and unconstitutional Federal Reserve, Fractional Reserve banking, and income tax on our citizens salaries, (3) who will stop trying to be the policeman of the world, (4) who will concentrate on a military whose main goal is to protect us from foreign invasion, and (5) a government that respects the sovereignty of the individual states.

With clarity of purpose and poignant concern, the author firmly states that the Federal Government violates our Constitution when it **indiscriminately** and **unjustifiably** involves itself in states' rights issues like, but not limited to, *No Child Left Behind*, *local law enforcement*, *drug enforcement*, *abortion issues*, and *federally controlled medical care*.

The unconstitutional *Patriot Act* and the *National Defense Authorization Act* was passed with barely a whimper from the public. These acts allow the federal government to accuse any American citizen of being a *Terrorist,* arresting them, incarcerating them and even assassinating them without benefit of legal representation or trial. Additionally, the United Nations sponsored *Agenda 21* is slowly but surely robbing the citizens of their property rights by masquerading as environmental issues.

Secrets of Our Hidden Controllers Revealed

This compelling book, in common language and with easy to read examples, explains why our country's monetary system does not need to be backed by gold or silver, and proposes a sample political platform that all our elected representatives need to adopt, regardless of their political affiliation.

The main purpose of the book is to encourage the reader to become better informed in order to elect those leaders who will return our great country to the one envisioned by our founding fathers.

Larry Flinchpaugh

About the author: John **Larry** Flinchpaugh was born April 16, 1939 in St. Joseph, Mo. and graduated from Central High School in 1957. He attended the University of Kansas, St. Joseph Junior College where he received an Associates of Arts degree, Missouri University extension in Kansas City, Mo. and later Tulsa University majoring in accounting. He was accredited by the International Accountants Society and worked for Phillips Petroleum Co. until April 1976. He then moved to Bakersfield, Ca. to work as an accounting manager for TOSCO. (The Oil and Shale Corporation)   In 1985 he semi-retired and with his wife and two sons started a company called Consign It Stores Inc. that specialized in liquidating estates for individuals, businesses and the Kern County Coroner's office. In 2005 he retired and returned to St. Joseph to be closer to his family and write about his experiences in searching for the truth regarding religious and political issues.

I would like to thank my loving wife Phyllis for all her help in proof reading, constructive criticism and typing of this book. Also thanks to my son Mark who wrote the "Preface" and was extremely helpful in critiquing and offering suggestions on the layout and organization of the material.

My goal in life is to become the person my dog thinks I am.
(Author Unknown)

J. Larry Flinchpaugh
March 2012

Table of Contents

Chapter One

My Quest for the Truth
(Pages 1-13)

Chapter Two

The Controllers of Public Opinion
(Pages 15-48)

Chapter Three

The Hegelian Dialectic
(Pages 49-52)

Chapter Four

9-11 Attack on the World Trade Center
(Pages 53-59)

Chapter Five

Religious Beliefs
(Pages 61-80)

Chapter Six

Political Beliefs
(Pages 81-94)

Chapter Seven

History of Money and Banking
(Pages 95-105)

Chapter Eight

Trial by Jury
(Pages 107-110)

Chapter Nine

The Draft Vs. A Voluntary Army
(Pages 111-113

Chapter Ten

Anti-Semitism
(Pages 115-124)

Chapter Eleven

Subliminal Warfare
(Pages 125-126)

Chapter Twelve

What Can You Do ?
(Pages 127-140)

Appendix

---Preface---
By
Mark Flinchpaugh

Art by: Fallyn Walker

Rumsfeld   Bush   Cheney

Who is controlling our "elected" leaders?

It is definitely **not** the American people.

Note April, 2009: Don't be fooled into believing that things have changed since we have a new Democrat, Obama administration in Washington. ***The exact same globalist puppet masters are still behind the scenes controlling everything.***

We the people of the United States, the citizens (the true government) are being assaulted by secretive and powerful international globalists from without and by corporofascist traitors from within. This elite group of arrogant, greedy men and women has attacked and jeopardized the freedoms of our once prosperous nation in their quest to establish a One World Government, a feudal state in which they will rule and we will serve!

You may ask yourself, "How can this be?" Have you noticed a deliberate and systematic loss of your freedoms and how our leaders continue to destroy our Constitution and Bill of Rights; our sovereign rights given to us by our Creator? This incremental process has come about so slowly that few realize that we have lost the liberties and rights we once had. Remember, once we relinquish our freedoms, they are difficult, if not impossible to restore.

We seem to have forgotten what made the United States of America great. More than 200 years ago our wise founding fathers set up a unique form of government, a Constitutional Republic of the people, by the people, and for the people. Three branches of government-the Executive, Legislative, and Judicial-were created with built-in checks and balances to prevent any one of them from acquiring too much power. The people had recently been under the tyrannical rule of King George the III of England and did not want that here. The Constitution required the Federal Government to be small, with certain well-defined duties and most of the powers and responsibilities to be delegated to the states or the people.

Today the Federal Government has grown to such a monstrous size that it no longer operates efficiently, economically and beneficially for **the people** but provides lifetime benefits for those who **once** promised to serve and protect this sovereign nation and its borders. Examples include the ineffective *War on Drugs, No Child Left Behind, border security, the irresponsible response to Hurricane Katrina and the excessive influence of corporate lobbyists.*

Most disturbing is that these past few years have seen the Executive branch ominously grab an enormous amount of power. 9-11 and the War on Terror has been the George W. Bush regime's excuse to assault our liberties and to trash our Constitution. George W. Bush, when sworn in as President, promised with a solemn oath, to preserve, protect, and defend the Constitution of the United States of America. But incredibly in November of 2005, he actually said, "Stop throwing the Constitution in my face, it's just a God damned piece of paper." (Capitol Hill Blue web site)

George W. Bush has signed **Presidential Directive 51** and other **Executive Orders** giving him sole authority to impose martial law and suspend Habeas Corpus. This gives him dictatorial powers over the people without any checks and balances.

The misnamed Patriot Act was hurriedly passed by Congress only **one month** after the 9-11 attack. Apparently it was written several months or maybe even years before 9-11. It appears that the authors of the bill either had advance knowledge of the attack or were just waiting to take advantage of it. The 9-11 attack against the United States was just what was needed to alter public opinion and encourage congress to approve of attacking Afghanistan and Iraq; an event that had been planned for some time. Some members later admitted that they didn't have time to read the entire bill. This abusive act permits:

(1) **secret** FBI searches of your home
(2) **secret** government wiretaps on your phone and internet
(3) **secret** investigations of your financial records
(4) **secret** searches of your library activities, medical, travel and business records
(5) the freezing of funds and assets without prior notice or appeal
(6) the creation of **secret** watch lists for airline travel and more.

The Military Commissions Act of 2006 and the 2012 NDAA, National Defense Authorization Act, gives the President the power to call any U.S. citizen an "enemy combatant", with the President defining what "enemy combatant" means. A citizen's simple criticism and dissent of our government's actions could be cast as 'treason' resulting in their arrest, property seizure and incarceration for life without a trial or lawyer. The Bush regime has even justified the use of torture to coerce 'confessions'.

The Bush administration has also violated the *Posse Comitatus Act* with the passing of the John Warner Defense Authorization Act of 2007. This act authorizes the President to declare an 'emergency' and to send Federal troops to a state, even if that states' Governor and citizens object. After Hurricane Katrina in New Orleans, the police and National Guard also violated the Second Amendment of our Constitution by confiscating law abiding citizens' guns that needed them for protection.

The propaganda arm of the Bush regime-the media corporations-have attempted to program and indoctrinate us to trust 'Dictator' Bush and surrender our constitutionally protected liberties so that he and Vice president Dick Cheney can protect us from the evil terrorists. This means our liberties are predicated only upon the grace of the Chief Executive—the president of the United States.

In the 1750's Benjamin Franklin printed the timeless and insightful quote, "Those who would give up essential Liberty, to purchase a little temporary Safety, deserve neither Liberty nor Safety."

The Federal government is rapidly diminishing every patriotic American's freedoms. The coming National ID cards with RFID (Radio Frequency Identification) chips embedded in them are not about fighting terrorism but all about controlling American citizens. In fact, tiny hidden spy chips are being planned for use in virtually every item on the planet for total 'Big Brother' surveillance and control.

Very alarming is the fact that Halliburton was given hundreds of millions of dollars for the construction of camps capable of holding a million people. The New York Times on February 4th, 2006 ran an article by Rachel L. Swarns entitled, *"Halliburton Subsidiary Gets Contract to Add Temporary Immigration Detention Centers."* The article states "KBR would build the centers for the Homeland Security Department for an unexpected influx of immigrants, to house people in the event of a natural disaster **or for new programs that require additional detention space.**"

In possible conjunction with this construction program, President George W. Bush could declare **Martial Law** against the American people and detain them in the event of an insurrection, as stated in the Military Commission Act of 2006. This massive act in Section 333 states, *"the President may employ the armed forces, including the National Guard in Federal service, to restore public order and enforce the laws of the United States when, as a result of a natural disaster, epidemic, or other serious public health emergency, terrorist attack or incident, **or other condition in any State or possession of the United States**, the President determines that domestic violence has occurred to such an extent that the constituted authorities of the State or possession are incapable of ("refuse" or "fail" in) maintaining public order, "in order to suppress, in any State, any **insurrection**, domestic violence, unlawful combination, or conspiracy."*

The government is afraid of the power of the people and appears to have very sinister plans for their total control.

The framework is all in place for this president or a future president to declare and implement total martial law and dictatorship. All that is needed is an 'emergency' event to occur, whether by happenstance or created.

Our founders gave us plenty of sound advice to protect our form of government. They warned us to obey the US Constitution with its checks and balances, because power corrupts.

They wanted us to keep our nation sovereign and independent. Yet the 'globalist elites' are destroying the United States with 'free trade' agreements like NAFTA and with the Security and Prosperity Partnership with Mexico and Canada. They are creating a North American Union with the ultimate goal of a One World Government. They are currently destroying the value of our dollar in order to bring about the new currency they call the Amero.

David Rockefeller, member of the Council on Foreign Relations and the Bilderberg Group supposedly admitted what the arrogant 'globalist' plan for the world is in the following quote from his book, '**Memoirs**', page 405-published by Random House, October 15, 2002. "Some even believe we are part of a secret cabal working against the best interest of the United States, characterizing my family and me as 'internationalists' and of conspiring with others around the world to build a more integrated global political and economic structure-one world government, if you will. If that is the charge, I stand guilty, and I am proud of it."

Our founders warned us about the dangers of foreign entanglements. A strong national defense is important but our **pre-emptive offensive wars** are damaging our nation. People around the world can see the unjustifiable aggression of the United States with the resulting millions of casualties. These wars are also crippling us economically by saddling our citizens and grandchildren with a growing National debt in 2012, of almost fifteen trillion dollars.

Our founders warned us of the dangers of allowing a private Central Bank (the Federal Reserve) to be in charge of our money, especially if it isn't backed by gold or silver. We have allowed these private bankers to print money out of thin air, loan it to us and charge us interest. And the creation of more and more money causes the devaluation of our dollar through inflation. Our government allows this fraud to continue because they can spend more money than they take in from taxes. The public has been fooled about the reality and origin of this hidden "inflation tax."

Our founders warned us of the importance of an honest, independent and unbiased press. Yet there is a small elite group of interlocking families and financial interests who rule America through their control of all the major newspapers, magazines, and broadcasting networks. Most of the public is not aware that they choose our politicians for us through their attention and promotion of some candidates and by ignoring and destroying other candidates. The 'Global elite' with the help of the media, control both parties, Democrat and Republican, to fool the public into believing they have a choice. Crises are continually being introduced or hyped to keep us in fear, to give up our rights for protection and for us to accept the 'New World Order'. Examples include computer hacking, gun crimes, AIDS, SARS, Bird Flu, Communism, 'Islamic-Fascist' terrorism, and global warming. We need to recognize that we are being manipulated for the benefit of the 'Global Elite' who wish to rule us as slaves. David Rockefeller once said, "We are on the verge of a global transformation. All we need is the right major crisis and the nations will accept the New World Order."

Our founders warned us that the price of liberty is eternal vigilance. Yet the ignorance and apathy of many citizens is obvious. We must remember that obeying the Constitution and the Bill of Rights is what makes America great. We must recognize that our rights and liberties are being destroyed. We need to remember that we created this government for **us** and we need not be afraid to restore it back to the great Constitutional Republic as originally founded.

Thomas Jefferson perhaps said it best when he said, "When the people fear the government, there is tyranny. When the government fears the people, there is liberty." In 1787 at the close of the Constitutional convention in Philadelphia, a woman asked Benjamin Franklin what kind of government had just been set up. He replied, "A Republic if you can keep it."

We must elect politicians who will follow the wishes of the people and not special interest groups that have no regard for what is best for our country. We must act quickly and decisively to return our great nation to the one our founding fathers intended.

The following book, written by my father, is profound and enlightening but simply and honestly written for everyone. It expands on the issues of our control by the elite with their hidden or deceptive tactics utilizing the media, government, schools, religious organizations and more. This book chronicles my father's journey for the truth and the meaning of life with interesting stories of personal experience, philosophy and humor.

Not only is there hope for personal spiritual growth but also hope for saving our great nation with many practical ideas presented.

I hope you will enjoy it as much as I did.

Mark Flinchpaugh

ELITE CONTROLLERS QUOTES

"In like manner, the scientific rulers will provide one kind of education for ordinary men and women, and another for those who are to become holders of scientific power. Ordinary men and women will be expected to be docile, industrious, punctual, thoughtless, and contented. Of these qualities probably contentment will be considered the most important. In order to produce it, all the researches of psycho-analysis, behaviorism, and biochemistry will be brought into play.... All the boys and girls will learn from an early age to be what is called 'co-operative,' i.e., to do exactly what everybody is doing. Initiative will be *discouraged* in these children, and insubordination, without being punished, will be scientifically trained out of them."
Bertrand Russell, 1931.

"There will be in the next generation or so **a pharmacological method of making people love their servitude and producing dictatorship without tears,** so to speak. Producing a kind of painless concentration camp for entire societies so that **people will in fact have their liberties taken away from them but will rather enjoy it,** because they will be distracted from any desire to rebel by propaganda, or brainwashing, or brainwashing enhanced by pharmacological methods. And this seems to be the final revolution."................................**Aldous Huxley, ca. 1960**

The ruling class has the schools and press under its thumb. This enables it to sway the emotions of the masses........**Albert Einstein**

I have sworn upon the alter of God, eternal hostility against every form of tyranny over the mind of man..........**Thomas Jefferson**

Introduction—

Throughout history, there have been the so called "elites" who suppress information and even lie and murder to further their agenda of controlling the masses. Still today, the government, the mass media and religious organizations are utilized by the elite for their selfish propaganda and oppressive control. Freedom, knowledge and innovation are stifled which retards the full potential of man. By seeking truth and knowledge we can break the chains of tyranny and make this a freer and happier world.

A book like the one you are reading can be written as a scholarly work or one simply written for the average person. A scholar can easily comprehend material written for the average person but the average person would not learn much from a scholarly work; mainly because they would most likely not even attempt to read it.

This is not a scholarly work; nor do I claim to be a scholar. Even if I were a scholar, I would still write this for the average person because what I have to share, in my opinion, is important enough to share with everyone, scholars and non-scholars alike. My discussions with college professors, who teach Government and Economics, and professionals such as attorneys and accountants, reveal how little even they know about our country's monetary policies, the Federal Reserve, constitutional law and the shaping of one's opinions through mind control.

It is important for me to point out here that a great deal of information presented in this book is only the author's opinion; however every effort was made to verify outside sources and facts presented. There is the possibility that I have made some errors but if so, these should not overly affect the main purpose of the book which is to encourage one to further research the important issues facing us today.

It is interesting for me to see how I have changed many of my own opinions in the last few years. Three years ago I was very critical of anyone who did not support President George Bush, Vice President Dick Cheney and Secretary of State Donald Rumsfeld.

After all, I thought, these are the leaders of our country and therefore we should respect and trust them. I now consider all three of these people as war criminals and believe they should have been impeached and if not impeached, be brought before the courts when they left office to face charges for war crimes. Making matters even worse, I have discovered that yes we get to **elect** the president of the United States but we don't get to **select** him. The elite controllers do that for us.

I Dare You!

I dare you to read this book and books like "The Christ Conspiracy-The Greatest Story Ever **Sold**" by Acharya S, "The Jesus Mysteries" by Timothy Freke and Peter Gandy and view the documentaries, "Zeitgeist", and "The Money Masters", and not become disturbed! If I have not irritated you, I have not accomplished my objective to get your attention and encourage you to get involved in a "**New Revolution of Thought.**"

Unfortunately, most people are simply too apathetic and too busy to get involved with new thoughts and ideas that would drastically change their **outdated** opinions. Most of the information presented in this book will more than likely be outside the readers "comfort zone."

Perhaps you think you already know all you need to know about religion and the important political issues facing us today. The revelations presented in this book may be shocking-but I sincerely hope it will open your eyes and expand your mind. This is more important than agreeing with the author on every issue.

Larry Flinchpaugh

Note Page:

Chapter One

My Quest for the Truth

Our Ailing Republic

Have you noticed the slow destruction taking place of our once great nation? Astute statesmen like Thomas Jefferson and Benjamin Franklin would be horrified to see that our President and Congress are completely disregarding the Constitution. Our founding fathers fought and died to preserve this country through the adoption of the United States Constitution rule of law. However, presidents like George W. Bush and Barack Obama see the Constitution as an impediment to their desire of dictatorial powers and use "Executive Orders" to constantly bypass it and the congressional oversight. Our Congress sits idly by while our Constitution is being ignored and our individual liberties are gradually disappearing with the passage of such laws as "The Patriot Act", "The Homeland Security Act.", "National Defense Authorization Act" (NDAA), and Obama Health Care.

Due to the controlled mass media propaganda, the failure of our educational system, and the outright lies of our political and religious leaders, most people are oblivious to what is really going on. The majority of those who **do** know feel that there is nothing they can do and have pretty well given up. Most feel that all they can do is to vote for the best political candidate based on the information they receive from the television evening news programs. They don't realize that these programs are designed more for entertainment and a means of altering the public's opinions. Even worse is when people vote for "the lesser of two evils", you still end up with evil. By becoming properly informed and getting involved in the political process, you **can** make a difference.

The Democrat and Republican Parties of our parents and grandparents generation no longer exist. The "hidden controllers" have gradually merged the two parties to where there is little difference today. It is more appropriate to call them the **Demopublicans** or the **Republicrats!** Jesse Ventura, former governor of Minnesota, even goes so far as to say, "We have a two party dictatorship."

Contrary to what Lou Dobbs of CNN thinks about registering as an independent, the necessary changes that will save this country must be made within the structure of our so called existing, two party system.

Registering and voting as an Independent historically does not produce the desired results. If we don't take action soon, I fear that the needed changes will only come about through bloodshed and the complete collapse of our existing system.

Beginning My Search for the Truth

While growing up in Saint Joseph, Missouri in the 1950's, my favorite thing to do was to talk to anyone who would listen. It didn't seem to matter to me that people weren't always interested in what I had to say. Why **wouldn't** everyone be interested in hearing about my new inventions and discoveries, seeing my coin and rock collection or hearing about how I had connected a toy telephone system from my attic to the basement? After all, I felt these discoveries and accomplishments were important and I merely wished to share them with others. As an adult, my basic philosophy of life still involves sharing what I have learned with others in hope that we can all improve our lives.

When I was about 18 years old, I made an important discovery but seldom do you meet anyone who has even heard of it. Have you ever gotten up in the middle of the night to get a drink of cold water from that water bottle in the refrigerator that you swore to your wife or mom that you never drink from? On the way to the refrigerator in the dark, you can see perfectly well because your eyes have adjusted to the dark, but when you open the door you are blinded by the bright light and have difficulty getting back to the bedroom in the dark. I discovered that just before opening the refrigerator door, close one eye. After you get your drink and close the door, open the closed eye. You can easily see with that eye to safely get back to the bedroom without running into anything. Doesn't everyone need to know about this important discovery?

I can honestly tell people that I grew up in a zoo. My father owned a pet shop, zoo and reptile gardens in St. Joseph, Missouri and it was my job to entertain our customers by giving them a guided tour and having our pet chimpanzee, Vicky Lynn, perform for them. One afternoon while I had Vicky out for a walk, I noticed a lady was attempting to get a coke from the coke machine but couldn't follow the simple directions as printed on the door. The instructions said (1) deposit dime in coin slot (2) push handle down (3) open door (4) remove bottle. Pretty simple but she was pulling the handle down before the coin had dropped down to release the bottle mechanism. I said to her, "Give me your dime and I will have Vicky get you the coke." Vicky put the dime in her teeth so it would easily fit into the horizontal slot and then she pulled the handle down, opened the door and removed the bottle. I looked at the lady and said, "See anybody can do it." She was not amused at my attempt to be humorous. I merely wanted to share with her my pet chimpanzee's intelligence.

Author's baby pet chimpanzee- "Vicky Lynn" on right. **"I should have taught Vicky sign language so I could have asked her if she believed in evolution."** *Note: both have a pacifier in their mouth!*

When I was 15 years old, I had to learn the Morse code to obtain a Ham Radio license from the Federal Communication Commission. At the time you were required to send and receive 13 words per minute using a telegraph key. It was really exciting for me as a teenager to be able to communicate with people around the world by sending and receiving messages, listening to the sounds of dots and dashes on a shortwave radio. Shortly after receiving my Ham Radio license, I heard a cricket chirping away and it sounded just like a Morse code message. I thought maybe "God" was attempting to communicate with me through the cricket. **(Remember I was only a 15 year old with a vivid imagination.)** I hurriedly found a piece of paper and pencil and began to write down the letters that the cricket was sending. He was going so fast that I had to write down the individual letters and later attempt to separate them into the proper words. I discovered that the cricket was not saying anything intelligible but did keep repeating the same series of letters over and over. I was disappointed to find that "God' was not trying to communicate with me through the cricket because that would have really given me something important to talk about.

Today, most of my friends would probably agree that I am even **more** annoying than I was in my youth; particularly since I have spent the last few years studying controversial religious and political issues. While intensely studying these issues, I came to the realization that we have been lied to and I have a strong desire to share this revelation with everyone I meet.

As I have gotten older, I find that it is difficult for me to hear as well as I used to and have discovered that it is sometimes safer for me to talk than it is to listen. My reasoning is, why take a chance on commenting on something that I may not have heard correctly? My wife says I have selective hearing and claims that I don't hear her when she asks me to take out the trash. But if she says, "Look, someone dropped a hundred dollar bill", I will always hear that! I think that what happens is that when a person with impaired hearing hears something that **sounds** important, they make a greater effort to listen. After all, taking out the trash is not nearly as important or as much fun as finding a hundred dollar bill.

As a child my father would say, "My God son, don't you ever shut up?" Now that I think about it, I believe that he liked to talk as much as I and maybe didn't like the competition. Most likely I inherited this trait from him; something that I do not believe is really that bad. I have found that you alienate some people when you talk a lot, but in the long run, one seems to make many more friends by being outgoing and sharing experiences with them. Since I have no hidden agendas, everyone I meet knows exactly where I stand. Therefore, not only do most people seem to appreciate that quality in me, I think they respect me for it. Some "Up Front" individuals have told me that, though they disagreed with my opinions, they still enjoyed our conversation. I took this as a compliment and feel that we both learned something from sharing our ideas.

Regardless of their opinion on a particular issue, I know that I have planted some seeds in their minds that will forever remain a part of their thought processes. When you think about it, this is a very important concept and you must be sensitive to the power this gives you in a way that will respect other's well-being.

Discussing Religious Beliefs

Perhaps you too have found that discussing religious beliefs with some people is not a good idea. One does not want to harm them emotionally; particularly since you may not be able to offer an alternative that is acceptable to them. Some may need their current belief system to be able to handle all their problems in life, and some because they are nearing the end of their life and are looking forward to everlasting life as described in the Bible. It would be very cruel and inconsiderate to attempt to remove a comfortable belief system from them.

As a youngster, I can still remember thinking, *What if I could discover the answers to the secrets of life? From where did I come? What is my purpose in life? What will happen to me after I die?*

Many of my Christian friends believe they have already discovered the answers to these questions and wish to share their beliefs with me. I sometimes envy those people who have found comfort from their particular religious beliefs but cannot help feeling that my religious beliefs are closer to the truth.

Albert Schweitzer has been quoted as saying, "At times our light goes out and is rekindled by a spark from another person. Each of us has cause to think with deep gratitude of those who have lighted the flame within us."

I know I have benefited from others sharing their views with me and I hope that people reading this book will benefit from examining and assessing my personal views and discoveries.

Like many others, I have a strong compulsion to discover the truth-- particularly about religion, philosophy and political issues-- and share it with others. However, most people are **not** interested or may feel uncomfortable discussing these subjects; many incorrectly believe that I want to share my views to gain their acceptance which will help validate my own opinions. This is definitely not the case.

I now understand how someone who has accepted Jesus Christ as their Lord and Savior feels when they try to share their experience with me and are disappointed or become frustrated when they can't convince me to adopt the same beliefs; particularly since their belief has given them so much comfort.

I explain that I am just as satisfied and comfortable with my religious beliefs as they are with theirs. If they persist, which I find somewhat disrespectful, I explain that I too was once where they are and have since then grown to where I am today. I only use this remark when I feel that they are attacking my views and refuse to even **consider** my point of view. I always hope they do not think too harshly of me for my religious opinions- but it is not an opinion that I came up with only recently. I have spent a great deal of time the last fifty or sixty years in studying and developing my personal belief system.

As an adult, I still like to talk and still incorrectly assume that everyone wants to listen. Many people would rather **not** listen and might even find my conversation annoying and somewhat depressing since most of them feel that there is nothing they can do to change things-plus they are comfortable with their current belief system.

One person, who was about my age of 70, told me that they had only another 10-15 years to live and did not want to worry about the things I talked about. They didn't want to think about (1) abolishing the private banking system called the Federal Reserve, (2) supporting our troops in Iraq by bringing them home immediately, (3) following the Constitution as the law of the land and (4) changing their religious beliefs.

In one instance, a friend politely asked me to shut up! Naturally I was a little offended but out of respect, I promptly complied and we have remained friends! I agree with what Thomas Jefferson said concerning this predicament, "*I never considered a difference of opinion in politics, in religion, in philosophy, as cause for withdrawing from a friend.*" It's too bad that everyone cannot adopt this attitude.

When discussing religion, philosophy and political issues, **many people are simply ignorant, lazy or too apathetic to care**. I know this sounds a little strong but I feel it is true. This attitude may be acceptable as long as it does not represent the voting majority of our population. However, if enough people do not inform themselves regarding the major issues that confront our nation and take steps to make changes, we will eventually lose the form of government and freedoms that our founding fathers fought so hard to establish. In fact we are already in the process of changing from a "Republic", which was established in 1776 by our founding fathers, to a "Democracy" that continually fails to abide by our Constitution. Our pledge of allegiance *still* says, "I pledge allegiance to the flag of the United States of America and to the *Republic* for which it stands........"and not to the *Democracy* for which it stands.

A friend once told me that he felt that I couldn't wait till he stopped talking so I could talk, and that I didn't need to feel like I had to fill in the blanks when he paused during a conversation. At first I took his criticism to be an insult but suddenly I realized his assessment was correct. Like many others, I find it difficult to listen to other people because I want to share with them my story or opinions before forgetting them; and of course my opinion is the correct one. I know this is wrong and may be interpreted as impolite. I continue to try and correct this flaw in my personality. Hopefully, I possess enough other positive traits to at least partially offset this negative one.

Sharing Experiences

By writing this book I hope to share some of my experiences and discoveries with people who want to listen by choice rather than by being trapped into a conversation with me. What I have discovered is that most all of us have been misled concerning the true workings of our government and religious organizations. Our educational system has made matters even worse by changing to a system of **training** its students instead of **educating** them. Animals are trained but humans should be educated. The Federal program "No Child left behind" aggravates this problem by training the students to simply pass the test. Sadly, individuals no longer learn to think critically and, thus fail to question the source of what they are taught. Was George Orwell correct in his novel, *1984, that some individuals or even large groups become little robots and are treated like Pavlov's dogs and laboratory rats:* Get the correct answer and you get a treat? (Federal money for local school programs) Get the wrong answers and get an electric shock? This is a classic example of the "dumbing down" of our educational system.

You will not find any school text books today that discuss such subjects as (1) the evils of our Federal Reserve System and Fractional Reserve Banking, (2) the differences between a "Republic" and a "Democracy" form of government, (3) Lysander Spooner's essay (1852) on the "Trial by Jury", (4) how foreign aid to third world countries is used to control them (5) how false religious doctrines have in many ways impeded human progress and is responsible for killing millions of people or (6) that Abraham Lincoln was wrong in not allowing the eleven southern states to secede.

In the appendix of this book is a list of quotes from famous Americans that seldom appear in the text books of today because they don't reflect the opinions and beliefs of the powerful controlling elite. I doubt you will find this quotation by Thomas Paine in any public school text books. *"All national institutions of churches, whether Jewish, Christian or Turkish, appear to me no other than human inventions, set up to terrify and enslave mankind, and monopolize power and profit"* or Thomas Jefferson's quotation, *"I have recently been examining all the known superstitions of the world, and do not find in our particular superstition (Christianity) one redeeming feature. They are all alike founded on fables and mythology."*

Also there is a list of biblical passages in the appendix that you most likely missed even if you have read the Bible thoroughly. Allegedly the Bible is the most widely "sold" book in the world but I would guess it is not the most "read" book in the world. Even if one has read the Bible, one probably finds a reason to dismiss those passages with which he disagrees. One might say, "Oh that is in the Old Testament, my church goes mainly by the New Testament" or "the Bible is merely a history of those people at the time of Jesus". Or even more ridiculous, "God is just testing our faith."

Why should one disregard the **Old** Testament when it appears that Jesus is saying in Mathew 5:17-18 that we are supposed to follow the Old Testament every "jot" and "tittle"? King James Version verse (17) *"Think not that I have come to destroy the law, or the prophets: I am not come to destroy but to fulfill. (*18) *For verily I say unto you, till heaven and earth pass, one jot or one tittle shall in no wise pass from the law, till all be fulfilled.*
Most Christians seem to "Cherry Pick" the Bible passages with which they agree and ignore the rest. For example, how many Christians actually believe if on your wedding night you find your

bride is not a virgin, you are supposed to kill her and put her body on her father's door step? (Deuteronomy 22: 13-21) Of course one could argue that this quote was taken out of context and doesn't really mean that literally. Trying to decide what it means literally opens up a whole new set of problems dealing with biblical opinions and interpretations. The Catholic Church at the Council of Trent (three sessions from 1545-1563) demanded that all Bible texts were to be taken literally insofar as possible. I guess that this one would fall under the category of, **"insofar as possible."**

I sincerely want to share some of my discoveries and hope that the more people learn and understand what is going on in the world concerning both government and religion, the more they will be able to help implement changes that will benefit us all. Maybe some will even be inspired enough to become leaders after getting closer to the truth concerning the important issues described in this book.

We have had few real leaders in our government who follow the will of the people since our founding fathers wrote the "Declaration of Independence", the "Bill of Rights" and the "Constitution." **Two recent exceptions to this would be Ron Paul, Republican Congressman from Texas and Dennis Kucinich, Democrat Congressman from Ohio.**

Ron Paul was repeatedly marginalized by the controlled mainstream media in the 2008 and 2012 presidential election for his views on abolishing the Federal Reserve System and on the need to stop being the policeman of the world. In Congressman Paul's address to the U.S. House of Representatives on September 10, 2002 he stated, "Mr. Speaker, I rise to introduce legislation to restore financial stability to America's economy by abolishing the Federal Reserve. I also ask unanimous consent to insert the attached article by Lew Rockwell, president of the Ludwig Von Mises Institute, which explains the benefits of abolishing the Fed and restoring the gold standard, into the record."

Ron Paul's vision is not as ridiculous as the controlled media wants you to believe. Thomas Jefferson got rid of the private central banking system and after it was again enacted, Andrew

Jackson also got rid of it. It was once again brought back in 1913 with the passage of the "Federal Reserve Act." It is no coincidence that the 16th Amendment was also passed at this same time authorizing income tax on our salaries. Even the famous economist, Milton Friedman has described the evils of our Federal Reserve System. William Jennings Bryan in his famous "Cross of Gold" speech in 1895, said...*"Those who are opposed to this proposition tell us that the issue of paper money is a function of the bank and the government ought to go out of the banking business. I stand with Jefferson rather than with them, and tell them as he did, that the issue of money is a function of the government and that the banks should go out of the governing business..."*

Ron Paul is in pretty good company when he says that the Federal Reserve should be abolished and the United States should return to constitutional monetary policies. Also Dennis Kucinich, Democrat Congressman from Ohio, has just recently called on the federal government to take back the power to issue money from the Federal Reserve.

Just because America has been a great country does not mean it will remain so. In fact our country is now sinking into the third world status as our economy fails with rising inflation and unemployment, and the trillion dollar government bailouts that will definitely not work. Millions of good paying manufacturing jobs have been lost to **unfair** free trade agreements such as NAFTA. We need **Fair** trade, not **Free** trade. This combined with the **Federal Income Tax** and the **hidden Inflation Tax** is slowly destroying the middle class. Eventually the **burden** of the working class supporting the non-working class will cause our entire system to collapse.

Encouraging Additional Research

At a minimum, I hope to stimulate the reader's thought processes and to encourage them to do additional research on the important issues confronting us today. For the first time in our history, the internet has made it possible for everyone to research any subject by giving them access to some of the greatest minds of the world.

Unfortunately many people today have not utilized this new and exciting technology with its unlimited potential.

Recently, I connected a lap top computer to my High Definition TV so that I could watch the new high quality video from the internet and listen to "Talk Radio" and view the corresponding video news clips on my TV. Imagine having your "Desk Top" on your large HD TV screen and being able to access it with a wireless keyboard from your recliner. It doesn't get any better than that! The last time anything like this happened that would increase mankind's ability to greatly enhance his knowledge was when Gutenberg invented the printing press around 1439.

It is much more comfortable to view video presentations on your TV instead of the small screen computer. Most likely future TV's will combine the TV and computer. However, with a little effort, one can do it now. If I miss something on TV, often others will record the program on the internet and display it on the fantastic web site, "You Tube" or "Google TV." Almost every day I talk to people who have never even heard of "You Tube" or know that there are web sites like "Snopes.com" which exposes hoaxes. Many of those informative emails you receive from your well intentioned friends are simply not true. In fact, just like your current news sources, all internet sources must be verified with multiple sources so one can be comfortable that the information is true and accurate. Even "Snopes" occasionally makes a mistake.

Some energetic and informed individuals have constructed web sites that will make math and money conversions, provide dictionary and encyclopedia references, translate languages from one to another, describe the various Bills before Congress, provide searchable biblical data bases, and allow one to listen to news and talk radio programs from around the world.

It is very interesting and informative to find out how the BBC (British Broadcasting Company) or "Al Jazeera" TV views Americas foreign policy. **I have found that the U.S. controlled media does not present the news with the same perspective as the foreign services.**

Secrets of Our Hidden Controllers Revealed

Is it possible that those in our government, who want the masses to remain ignorant on certain issues, view the internet as a threat to their abusive agenda? As time goes on, I fear that the government will interfere with the freedom we now have to gather and disseminate knowledge through the internet; most likely the argument will be that they are protecting us from the **"Terrorists."** I certainly hope that this doesn't happen. However, I think that some internet providers have already blocked information that our government has labeled as a threat to national security when in fact it has nothing to do with national security.

We should all be watching very closely the new high speed fiber optics Internet2 program being developed for our government and universities and the changes the Canadian internet providers are considering. It is expected that in the near future, internet providers will be charging additional fees to access certain web sites. This is a very subtle way of blocking web sites which the government feels the citizens should not access. Some of these changes would ultimately eliminate independent web sites with the "elites" deciding which sites you need to get your information.

We must be ever vigilant to thwart the "elite" controller's plan of slowly destroying our personal freedoms and our country's sovereignty.

"A wise man makes his own decisions; an ignorant man follows public opinion"—Chinese proverb

"Do not choose to be wrong for the sake of being different."—Lord Samuel

"Don't judge a man by his opinions, but by what his opinions have made him."—G. C. Lichtenberg

German Nazi Politician

*"It is the absolute right of the state to supervise the Information of public opinion."—**Joseph Paul Goebbels**,*

(Authors note: Sadly to say, this is currently happening in the United States.)

Chapter TWO
The Controllers of Public Opinion

Controlling the opinions of the masses through "thought control" and "mind control" is relatively easy; especially when it is allowed to incrementally increase over several generations. People do not even realize it is happening to them. It is like the story of putting a frog in cold water and gradually turning up the heat to cook him. The frog doesn't jump out because he does not notice the slow increase in heat. It is time for the American people to jump out of the water now before it is too late.

Most of us are lazy, ignorant of the facts, and apathetic when it comes to understanding the really important issues facing us today. For example, most people have been taught to believe that we are governed primarily by the three branches of government; the Executive, Legislative, and Judicial system and that these separations of power protect us with what is called "The Balance of Power." Our founding fathers wisely set up this system to protect us citizens from a tyrannical government. At least, that is what we have all been taught in school. I have discovered it isn't working that way at all today.

The Banksters

There is actually a hidden level **above our elected officials,** who were not elected nor are they accountable to the people; they are sometimes referred to as "The Banksters" or "Shadow Government". These private elitist bankers not only control our money supply and interests rates, but also our economy, foreign policy, the amount we pay for our homes and automobiles and whether or not we have a job. With their virtually unlimited supply of money, they have bought control of the mass media, political parties, and the military industrial complex companies. They even control the boom and bust business cycle.

Contrary to popular belief, the business cycle (Periods of prosperity, inflation, deflation and depression) is not an accident.

The elite bankers not only control the cycle but know how to work the system to their financial benefit; especially with advance knowledge as to what they are going to do regarding interest rates and the money supply. They know exactly when to buy or sell real estate and dump their stock so they can buy it back at pennies on the dollar. The average American citizen cannot take advantage of this private and privileged information unless it is simply by accident.

I accidentally made a handsome profit on a house I purchased in California in 1976 for $50,000 and sold it in 2004 for $275,000. I merely rode on the coat tails of the "Banksters" immoral banking system. Many Americans were not able to take advantage of this corrupt money system unless they had invested in real estate or other inflation sensitive assets such as gold, silver, certain stocks, etc.

The Banksters include such powerful people as the Rockefellers and the Rothschilds. Their immoral and unconstitutional banking policies cause the rich to get richer and the poor to get poorer each time we go through a boom and bust period. An important point to remember is that when we experience a recession or depression, **wealth is not lost.** It is merely transferred from the poor and middle class to the rich. This has been going on since the founding of our Republic in 1776. In fact, the bankers and money changers have been controlling and taking advantage of the ignorant and apathetic masses since ancient times. Do you remember the story of how Jesus drove out the money changers from the temple in Jerusalem 2,000 years ago?

The Banksters do not care if the current occupant of the White House is a Republican or a Democrat because they control both parties. The patriarch of the Rothschild banking dynasty, Mayer Amschel Rothschild (1744-1812) once said, *"Give me control of a nation's money and I care not who makes its laws."*

Our government has gone back and forth from a government controlled monetary system, as provided by our Constitution, to a privately controlled central bank or as it is called today, the

Federal Reserve System. Our most recent mistake in adopting a private central banking system was the passing of the Federal Reserve System Act in 1913. It was passed under some very questionable circumstances. The bankers, who had secretly written this act for **their benefit**, publically complained that they did not like it. The public was thus fooled into believing that this act would reign in the excessive power of the bankers. Most of the congressmen had gone home for the Christmas holidays and were not even aware that such an important bill was to be voted on.

The income tax on peoples' salaries was also started in 1913 with the passage of the 16th Amendment; which provided funds to pay the private Federal Reserve bankers for interest they charge us for printing and loaning our government our own money. This immoral banking system has proven to be very profitable for the "Banksters" but extremely detrimental to the average citizen.

Contrary to its original promises to do so; ever since 1913 the Federal Reserve has done a **terrible** job in protecting our economy and the wealth of the common citizen. The Federal Reserve's monetary policies contributed to the 1929 crash and actually prolonged the depression. The Banksters then manipulated us into WWII, which helped to end the depression, but thousands of Americans lost their lives in this unnecessary war. The Federal Reserve's policies were also responsible for the recessions of the late 1980's, early 2000's and now the approaching depression or severe recession.

It is no coincidence that those leaders opposing the privately owned central bank have been targets of assassination or plots to end their political career. (Abraham Lincoln, Andrew Jackson, James Garfield, Congressman Louis T. McFadden, John F Kennedy and others)

Louis McFadden, a true servant of the people, was a Republican congressman from 1920-1931 and Chairman of the House Banking and Currency Committee during the Great Depression. He had many political and banking enemies which most likely caused his life to be cut short. He had claimed that Jews controlled the American economy-- "The gentiles have the slips of paper while the Jews have the lawful money." He accused the Federal Reserve of deliberately causing the depression and he claimed Wall Street bankers funded the 1917 Bolshevik Revolution through the Federal Reserve Banks and the European Central Banks. In 1932 he moved to impeach President Herbert Hoover, and also introduced a resolution bringing conspiracy charges against the "Board of Governors" of the Federal Reserve. There were two attempts to assassinate him- first a failed shooting and second in 1936 an apparent poisoning that made him violently ill and caused his death.

The elite banking interests which have control over the masses of people use a subtle form of "Thought Control" by keeping most of their operations a secret. Any political leaders today who would decide to work towards abolishing the Federal Reserve or question the real "power behind the throne" should do so only as a large group and should be sure not to fly together on the same airplane. Paul Wellstone, a Democrat who spoke out against war with Iraq and who was one of the few congressmen calling for an independent investigation of the 9-11 attacks, died in a plane crash along with his wife and daughter, three staff members and two pilots on October 25, 2002. There have been many suspicious plane crashes that have taken the lives of several of our congressmen. It is difficult to prove any wrong doing in these accidents but they do appear to be highly suspicious.

This process of control by the elite over the ignorant, lazy, or apathetic masses has been in existence for thousands of years. The Egyptian Pharaohs could control their people with the knowledge they had of the astronomical laws which could predict such events as the flooding of the Nile River and seasonal changes, and mathematical knowledge that gave them the ability to build the pyramids. The ignorant masses could easily be held subservient to this well-educated class of forceful leaders. In this simple example of "Control", it is the control of the educated over the uneducated. Nothing sinister here but let's look at how it is done in modern times.

Today, the concept of "Thought Control" or as some describe it as "Mind Control", becomes a little more sophisticated. I tend to think of "Thought Control" as controlling the masses opinions and "Mind Control" as the control of a particular individual to perform a clandestine act such as an assassination or sabotage. There are opposing views on whether "Mind Control" is even possible. Many believe that Mind Control is just another conspiracy theory-even though there **is** evidence of its existence.

Conspiracy Nut and Anti-Semitic Labels

Why does the mass media and organizations like the Anti-Defamation League of B'nai B'rith (ADL) continue to label individuals who attempt to expose what is going on today as "Conspiracy Nuts" or "Anti-Semitic?"   This can usually be understood as a ploy to marginalize the messenger. When the public hears that someone has been called a "Conspiracy Nut", or "Anti-Semitic" they have been preconditioned to totally disregard both the message and the messenger! These two terms have been used very effectively by those in control to silence their opposition.

For example, when TV personalities such as Bill O'Reilly or Sean Hannity (Fox News) have someone on their show who is not well informed on something like the "9-11 attack conspiracy theories", they will marginalize their guest by calling him a "Conspiracy Nut." Once the host has labeled him a "Conspiracy Nut", the listener has been programmed in a negative way to disregard anything the guest might say; it doesn't matter if he is telling the truth.

I wrote a letter to one of the TV personalities to suggest that they might want to invite guests like Lieutenant Colonel Robert Bowman, PHD, United States Air force (ret), or former U.S. Air Force pilot Lieutenant Jeff Dahlstrom to challenge the official account of 9-11. Of course they would not invite someone of this caliber to appear on their show because it would not be as easy to discredit him.   Most hosts of the TV programs have a preconceived idea about 9-11 and choose to not even consider the guests' views if they are different from theirs or if the guest suggests that there may have been rogue elements within our own government that participated in the attack. This marginalizing of people trying to expose the truth is quite troubling. The average citizen doesn't even realize it is happening. The next time you hear the media or the Anti-Defamation League (ADL) use the terms **"Conspiracy Nut"** or **"Anti-Semitic,"** you might want to look very closely at what they are really saying in order to discover their true agenda.

When you are mislabeled by someone calling you a 'Conspiracy Nut" or "Anti-Semitic" because of your views, you should demand that your accuser define these terms. Once the terms are defined and agreed upon by both parties, there may not be any argument after all. To make my point, I have often used the example about the tree falling in the forest. If there is no one there to hear it fall is there any sound? It is futile to try to answer this question until you define the word "sound". If your definition of sound is a vibrating body like a tuning fork, a medium to transfer the vibrations like air or water, and a receiver to pick up the sound, then of course there is no sound by this definition because there is no one there to receive or hear it. But if, in your definition, you exclude the receiver, there is "sound." It's pretty simple once you agree on the definition of terms. If you cannot nullify the attack by defining the terms then you should openly and forcibly accuse the attacker of attempting to conceal the truth by using this unfair labeling ploy.

Thought and Mind control

"Thought Control" (Control of the Masses) & "Mind Control" (Control of Individuals) can be initiated by:

(1) Brute Force (2) Propaganda (3) Religious Doctrine (4) Indebtedness (5) Withholding scientific knowledge (6) Molestation and mistreatment of children and adults (7) Hunger (8) Drug Addiction (9) Use of mind altering drugs.

Brute Force

Brute force is probably the oldest and most effective example of control. In prehistoric times, the cave man with the biggest club pretty well dictated what the weaker ones would do and think! In modern times, Dictators like Stalin and Hitler were also very efficient in controlling the minds of their people. If you didn't go along with the states' program, you were either put in prison or put to death. A recent example of Brute Force would be "Water Boarding" as used by the United States on the imprisoned, so called, **"terrorists."**

Propaganda

One of the most widely used forms of "Thought Control "to alter and guide public opinion today is through the use of propaganda. (Deceptive or distorted information that is designed to secretly influence people.) It is mainly abused by the controlled monopolistic mainstream media, government political speeches, and press releases to the media.

The media has several ways of manipulating public opinion. Once you are aware of these tactics, you should be in a much better position to separate fact from fiction. Some methods they use are:

Labels—Use of labels like "Conspiracy Nut", "Anti-Semitism", "Evil Doers", "Paranoid", etc are used by the media very effectively to discredit or silence the opposition. We have been programmed by them to react predictably in negative ways when we hear these terms.

Exaggeration—"Global Warming" is probably the best example. When the media is interviewing a so called expert on this subject, you should ask yourself, what is the agenda and what is the back ground of the person being interviewed? Are these people's views from a religious, political, environmentalist or a research scientist standpoint? Also it would be helpful to know if the expert being interviewed worked for the government or worked for a company that had lucrative contracts with the government. Does this so called expert have any financial interests in the issue being reported; i.e. is he or his country going to profit from selling "Carbon Credits?"

Discredit—the use of a spokesperson or announcer to make one of them look unbiased and the other to look biased. Fox Network's "Hannity and Colmes" is an example of this method.

Censorship—the reporter or editor censors the news he doesn't like. This was obvious when Ron Paul was running as a presidential candidate. Although Ron Paul's views appealed to a huge percentage of the American population, he received minimal air time.

Perception Distortion—Failure of journalists to apply critical scrutiny to favored people or causes. A few years ago Katie Couric was interviewing a guest and talking about Arnold Schwarzenegger, who was running for Governor of California. She made the comments, "I wonder if the public knows that Arnold's father was a Nazi, or that he is known as a womanizer, and has been reported takings steroids?" When it came time to discuss his opponent, she was much less critical.

Headline Positioning—Many readers only see the headline and therefore may have a distorted view of the relevance of the story. The editor can alter the reader's opinion simply by making use of the location of the headline. The headline can be on page one or page 32 or it can be next to another headline that draws more attention to it than if it were surrounded by say advertising or the comics.

Acceptable Lies—describing something that **may not** be true but is widely **accepted** as true because it is stated repeatedly. An example of this is when the media continually refers to the "Palestinian Homeland". The Palestinians never had a "homeland." I guess it might be partially true if they referred to them as the "Palestinian **Arab** Homeland." What about the "Palestinian Christian Homeland?" Actually the **Arab** Palestinians already have a Palestinian homeland called Jordan. When the Ottoman Empire was broken up after WW l, one third of the area went to Israel (west of the Jordan River) and two thirds went to the Arabs (east of the Jordan River) and was called Trans Jordan.

Positioning—placing news items near other news to add additional meaning to the facts. i.e. budget cuts news next to homeless stories.

Misrepresenting Opinions for Facts—the writer or speaker makes statements by quoting people who agree with them and treats these statements as if they were facts instead of opinions.

Overstating Your Opponents' Position-- the good guys are labeled with words such as "moderate" or "freedom fighters" and the bad guys are labeled as "extremists" or "terrorists." This method is also described as a "Straw Man" argument where there is a misrepresentation of an opponent's views. The use of this method deliberately overstates the opponent's position.

The propaganda in the media can be difficult to detect because of the subtleties used. Most often it just appears to be the bias of the announcer or editor.

A quick look at the world wide news being reported from other countries (e.g. the Al Jazeera web site) will open your eyes to the fact that there are many countries and news organizations that have different views on news pertaining to the U.S. It is not that difficult to find multiple news sources from around the world that will enable you to be better informed.

In the 1950's, I remember my excitement buying a shortwave radio from Acme Radio that received an English language news program from Russia. It was interesting to note the differences in each country's views and trying to determine which one was telling the truth.

As a college student I had to write a term paper that would be a large part of my grade. Therefore, I needed a subject that would be so clever and interesting that even if I did not write it very well, the professor would give me a good grade just for the idea. I decided to write several different newspapers in different parts of the United States and request that they all send me a copy of their paper on the same day so I could compare a national news story and determine if they had reported it fairly.

Fortunately, I had chosen the day Martin Luther King was arrested in a demonstration in the South. The southern newspaper had King's story on the front page with a large picture of him being thrown into a police "paddy wagon". The headlines of the story were huge. **"King Arrested in Demonstration"**. The Des Moines, Iowa paper had the same story on page six with a file postage stamp size picture of Mr. King dressed in a suit and tie and the headline was **"King Detained"**. The East and West coast papers had varying degrees of differences somewhere in between the paper in the South and the paper in Iowa.

It was interesting to see how the same news story could be portrayed differently because of the reader's geographic location and the attitude of the editors **and** the readers.

It should be obvious that one needs to have multiple sources of information so they can get closer to the truth; which will make it more difficult for those in power to purposely lie to us. We should make it as difficult as possible for them to control our opinions with false information.

Fox News: <u>Un</u>-Fair and <u>Un</u>-balanced

After seeing how the TV networks marginalized Congressmen Ron Paul in the 2008 and 2012 presidential race, I have come to the conclusion that Fox is not as fair and balanced as they so proudly claim. If one paid close attention on how they covered the presidential candidates, you may also agree with my assessments.

They excluded Republican Congressman Ron Paul and Representative Duncan Hunter in 2008 from the New Hampshire debate. They included the top five candidates, Mike Huckabee, Mitt Romney, Rudy Giuliani, John McCain and Fred Thompson- even though most of the Polls showed that Ron Paul had a better chance of winning than Fred Thompson.

If you have ever watched "Hannity and Colmes" and heard Sean talk about Ron Paul, it would be obvious that he is not being "Fair and Balanced." Sean was telling his viewers what a great job Fox News was doing in conducting one of their presidential candidate polls, but when Ron Paul won the poll, Sean made a comment that the poll in this case was inaccurate because all the internet fans of Ron Paul had skewed the results by massive call ins. I guess no other candidate's support groups would have stooped so low as to support their candidate with massive call ins. One of Ron Paul's supporters admitted that he tried to call in twice but got a recording that only one vote per telephone number would be accepted. So much for Sean Hannity's analysis on why Congressman Paul won!

When one continually hears Fox TV personalities like Hannity and guests like neoconservative Bill Kristol from the "Weekly Standard" refer to Congressman Ron Paul as a fringe candidate with no chance of winning, one need not wonder about the true agenda of FOX News and the Weekly Standard.

Do a Google search of Bill Kristol and his father, Irving Kristol, if you would like to get a better in depth view of Fox Networks views and agenda. To get a better in depth view of Congressman Ron Paul, do a Google search on "You Tube" for Ron Paul. You will find that Congressman Paul represents 70% of the electorate who are dissatisfied with the President and congress. So why wasn't he given more air time?

As Sheppard Smith of FOX News says 'We Report, You Decide." I have decided, FOX News is definitely not "Fair" nor is it "Balanced."

Other Media Bias

A media outlet that favors Hillary Clinton may give her press coverage 100 times in a week compared to Ron Paul whom they mention only 5 times in a week. They can honestly say they covered both candidates. In the 2008 presidential race, Ron Paul was constantly marginalized by all the networks. Ron Paul was the only presidential candidate who promised to bring our troops home immediately from not only Iraq but other bases around the world, to abolish the Federal income tax on individuals and to return to a government that abides by the Constitution. This should have been "Big" news! This was a revolution in the Republican Party platform and American politics, but you heard very little about it in the controlled lame stream press.

Following is a transcript, from the Congressional record, of Congressman Paul's speech on February 7, 2007 to Congress regarding Income Tax:

"Madam Speaker, I am pleased to introduce the Liberty Amendment, which repeals the 16th Amendment, thus paving the way for real change in the way government collects and spends the people's hard-earned money. The Liberty Amendment also explicitly forbids the federal government from performing any action not explicitly authorized by the United States Constitution.

The 16th Amendment gives the federal government a direct claim on the lives of American citizens by enabling Congress to levy a direct income tax on individuals. Until the passage of the 16th amendment, the Supreme Court had consistently held that Congress had no power to impose an income tax.

Income taxes are responsible for the transformation of the federal government from one of limited powers into a vast leviathan whose tentacles reach into almost every aspect of American life. Thanks to the income tax, today the federal government routinely invades our privacy, and penalizes our every endeavor.

The Founding Fathers realized that "the power to tax is the power to destroy," which is why they did not give the federal government the power to impose an income tax. Needless to say, the Founders would be horrified to know that Americans today give more than a third of their income to the federal government.

Income taxes not only diminish liberty, they retard economic growth by discouraging work and production. Our current tax system also forces Americans to waste valuable time and money on compliance with an ever-more complex tax code. The increased interest in flat-tax and national sales tax proposals, as well as the increasing number of small businesses that question the Internal

Revenue Service's (IRS) "withholding" system provides further proof that America is tired of the labyrinthine tax code. Americans are also increasingly fed up with an IRS that continues to ride roughshod over their civil liberties, despite recent "pro-taxpayer" reforms.

Madam Speaker, America survived and prospered for 140 years without an income tax, and with a federal government that generally adhered to strictly constitutional functions, operating with modest excise revenues. The income tax opened the door to the era (and errors) of Big Government. I hope my colleagues will help close that door by cosponsoring the Liberty Amendment."

CNN's Jeffrey Toobin sarcastically made the remark that Mike Huckabee and Ron Paul actually wanted to abolish the IRS. Toobin then made the remark, "How can we run our government without tax revenues?" Everyone on the panel laughed and snickered including Bill Bennett. Most listeners probably accepted the idea that Mike Huckabee and Ron Paul were complete idiots and had views that were not compatible with the mainstream Republican philosophy. Is Toobin really that stupid? Is he just not well informed or were his remarks following the dictates of his network's management? A study a few years ago showed that most taxes collected by the IRS on peoples salaries do not go to pay for services for the people at all but rather pays mainly for the interest the privately run Federal Reserve System charges the American public for printing and loaning us our own money.

I believe Mike Huckabee wanted to abolish the IRS and replace our individual income tax with a flat tax and Ron Paul wanted to abolish it and not replace it with anything. When one is required to pay income tax on his salary, it can be considered a **form of slavery** and some have even pointed out that it is unconstitutional. In effect you are simply trading your labor for money. Why should this be taxable? You would still need to have the IRS administer the collection of taxes on corporate and business profits and on capital gains on real estate and stocks and bonds- which **is** constitutional and necessary to finance many of our government's legitimate programs.

There definitely would be no need for an income tax on our salaries if the Federal Reserve System was abolished and the United States stopped trying to police the entire world. Bringing our troops home from many of the military bases around the world would alone save us enough to balance the Federal Budget in just a few short years. It has been estimated that we have over 700 military bases in over 130 countries throughout the world. Just think how much improvement could be made to your living standard if we did not have the expense of policing the world and were not required to pay income taxes on our salaries. How much better off would you and your community be if every citizen received a 15-20% raise?

During several CNN interviews, Lou Dobbs gave Congressman Ron Paul (R-Tex) the degree of respect he deserves but later Mr. Dobbs kept telling his viewers that he and everyone else should leave the Republican and Democrat parties and register as an Independent. He continues to claim that no one in the current administration is running the country as it should. Did Mr. Dobbs forget about his interview with Ron Paul? Lou Dobbs continually blames our Representatives and President for the failures of our foreign and domestic policies but fails to recognize the fact that Congressman Paul is willing to make the changes necessary to cure our sick country. Why wouldn't Mr. Dobbs support Congressman Paul? It makes one wonder about the true agenda of CNN.

Sometimes the media simply ignores important stories and emphasizes stories about murder, rape, and celebrity gossip. A relevant story that is ignored is about as bad as an outright lie! Benjamin Franklin once said, **"Half a truth is often a great lie."**

Just recently the 2008 "Bilderbergers" meeting was held near Washington DC, apparently discussing subjects like, whether the U.S. should bomb Iran, what to do about the high gasoline prices and how to correct the disaster of our monetary policies. You would think this meeting attended by the world's leaders would have been covered by the news media. Neither my local newspaper nor TV station covered this story and when contacted by phone, advised me that they had never heard of the "Bilderbergers." Our local newspaper like thousands of papers subscribes to the *Associated Press* (AP) which you would think would have a story about this important meeting of world leaders. The following quote by David Rockefeller, a Bilderberg member, explains why. He was once quoted as saying, *"We are grateful to the Washington Post, The New York Times, Time Magazine and other great publications whose directors have attended our meetings and respected their promises of discretion for almost forty years. It would have been impossible for us to develop our plan for the world if we had been subjected to the lights of publicity during those years. But, the world is now more sophisticated and prepared to march towards a* **world government**. *The supranational sovereignty of an intellectual elite and world bankers is surely preferable to the national auto-determination practiced in past centuries."* Don't let anyone tell you that the idea of a **One World Government** is a Conspiracy Theory.

A quick internet search of the Associated Press board members showed that media mogul Rupert Murdoch (a Bilderberg member) was on their board. This pretty well explains why it was kept secret. The "Logan Act" makes it unlawful for any public official to attend a secret meeting where world policies are decided. It appears that there is no one who wants to enforce this law.

Government propaganda: Bush, Cheney and Rumsfeld lied about Weapons of Mass Destruction in Iraq, lied concerning the 9-11 Commission Report, and lied about Iran and Venezuela being our enemies. The Warren Report, about the Kennedy assassination, the Gulf of Tonkin incident in 1964, and Israel's **so called** "accidental" attack in 1967 of the USS Liberty ship were also lies. These continuing incidences of lying make it more and more difficult to believe our government's explanation of political events occurring in the world today.

If you are not aware of these lies or believe they are just more conspiracy theories, I suggest you start researching the topics discussed in this book. There is an abundance of literature and web sites available that will give you much more data to properly assess the truthfulness of these important incidences.

It is extremely irresponsible and I personally think criminal for the news media **to not** expose these lies and exaggerations by our government. The media is more concerned about profits, providing the people with entertainment and protecting their elite friends than reporting the truth in world affairs.

Currently the Obama administration, the controlled main stream news media and the Israeli lobbyists are doing everything possible to make the American public believe that the U.S. must make a preemptive strike against Iran. "Preemptive" strike in this case really means aggressive, unconstitutional and unwarranted strike. If John McCain had been elected president, he would most likely have continued Bush's policy of "Preemptive Strikes" against our so called "enemies" without congressional approval. How can Iran be our enemy when Iraq's present government has diplomatic relations with Iran? Could our foreign policy in the Middle East be contributing to the Iranians possible involvement in supporting the terrorists? Just who are the terrorists anyway; Al Qaeda or the United States government who has killed over a million Iraqi citizens? As Barack Obama's former pastor, Reverend Wright said, "The chickens will come home to roost." Contrary to what the controlled press wants you to believe, there is a lot of truth in what the pastor is saying.

There are many Americans who believe the 9-11 commission has not told the truth on what really happened that fateful day. Following are just a few of the unexplained questions. (1) Why did World Trade Center building seven collapse at nearly free fall speed when it wasn't even struck by an airplane? (2) How do you explain that several of the hijackers have recently been seen alive? (3) How could our government have names and pictures of the hijackers the very next day? (4) If our government was that efficient, why wasn't it able to prevent the 9-11 attack? (5) Why weren't the hijackers' names on the airlines passenger lists? (6) Why did the collapse of the twin towers look like a controlled demolition with numerous reports of bombs going off inside? (7)

Why wasn't there a type of engine found at the Pentagon that matched the type of plane that supposedly hit the Pentagon? (8) How could there have been molten steel when airplane fuel will not burn hot enough to melt steel? (9) How in the world could the massive "Patriot Act" be written and passed by both Houses of Congress only one month after the 9-11 attack. (10) Why were many of the "hijackers" cleared for entry into the United States as government operatives and trained at U.S. military bases? (11) Why did the 9-11 commission state that determining who funded the attacks had little or no value?

It looks like someone had prior knowledge that such an event was going to happen. I have not heard of any legitimate answers to these questions. The documentaries, "Loose Change" and "9-11 Ripple Effect" expose many of the questions that the 9-11 Commission either failed to address or failed to give plausible answers.

Don't the American people deserve to know the truth as to what really happened? Another investigation should be made by an **independent** group to answer the conspiracy theorists questions and to punish those responsible. If you don't believe that rogue elements of our government were involved in some way or had prior knowledge that 9-11 was going to happen, you are a perfect example of someone who is not well informed. Several members of the original 9-11 investigative commission have just recently expressed their doubts as to the final conclusions of the report. Do your research and then decide; don't allow the controlled mass media to be your only source of information. Albert Einstein said, *"Condemnation without verification is ignorance."*

The 9-11 attack is not the first time our government has failed to tell the American people the truth. Most Americans don't believe the Warren Commission Report concerning President Kennedy's assassination. In my opinion Lee Harvey Oswald was the "patsy"; just like Sirhan Sirhan, Timothy McVeigh and the 19 Arab hijackers. Shouldn't it be considered a little odd and a conflict of interest to have had Allen Dulles head up the Warren Commission? Remember John Kennedy had fired Allen Dulles as head of the CIA and the CIA was suspected of being involved in the assassination. When you realize all the powerful enemies that Kennedy had, it does not seem likely that someone like Oswald was a lone assassin.

Let's look at some of Kennedy's enemies. First and most important, President Kennedy had made it clear to Israel that he would not allow them to become a nuclear power. I am sure Ben Gurion was extremely upset at this and used the Israeli Mossad to do everything in its power to get nuclear weapons. As mentioned earlier Allen Dulles was fired as head of the CIA. It is alleged the New York crime syndicate helped get Kennedy elected and then President Kennedy and his brother Bobby launched an investigation against the mob. Vice President Johnson was being investigated for possible campaign contribution fraud. J Edgar Hoover, head of the FBI, was most likely to be replaced by Kennedy. Fidel Castro didn't appreciate the assassination attempts by the U.S. on his life. The American banking elites did not like the fact that Kennedy had bypassed the Federal Reserve System, even though he was abiding by the Act of 1878, by printing millions of dollars of interest free treasury notes, effectively eliminating the Federal Reserve of collecting interest on these particular notes. This act was a mandate by congress that a certain number of Treasury Department notes always had to be in circulation. Many people believe that Kennedy recognized the evils of the Federal Reserve and had long term plans to abolish this corrupt and unconstitutional monetary system.

With all of these people hating Kennedy, it is easy to see why he was assassinated. The problem was to keep the details a secret and figure out how to blame it on someone other than the true perpetrators. So far those responsible have done a pretty good job of keeping it a secret. Who would have had the expertise and financing behind them to carry out such a clandestine operation other than rogue elements in the American CIA, FBI and the Israeli Mossad?

Our government also lied to us about being attacked by the North Vietnamese in the gulf of Tonkin in 1964 for the purpose of escalating the war in Vietnam. One of my high school friends was there and said that they were woken up in the middle of the night and were told to fire into the dark- even though no one was firing at them! The next day Johnson lied, stating the U.S. had been attacked by the North Vietnamese. There have been previously classified documents made available that support this charge of fabrication.

On June 8, 1967 the Israeli government maliciously and deliberately attacked the USS Liberty reconnaissance ship in the international waters off the Sinai Peninsula near Egypt. They used unmarked planes and vessels to launch the attack against our ship that was clearly flying the American flag. Thirty four American servicemen were murdered and at least 173 wounded. An inquiry was made but again our government lied to us. "It was all a mistake" the report said and Israel apologized. The American sailors were threatened to not discuss the matter with anyone. They feared that their pensions would be suspended and may even be killed if they discussed what really happened. Some believe it was Israel's intention to leave the impression that the U.S. had been attacked by Egypt so the U.S. would then retaliate by attacking Egypt. This would have made it much easier for Israel to win the Arab Six Days War with Egypt, Jordan and Syria. As it turned out Israel didn't need our help.

This unprovoked Israeli attack on an American ship is what is called a "False Flag" operation; a term used to blame some-one else other than the actual perpetrator. It almost worked in this case. If a Russian ship had not passed nearby it is believed that Israel would have killed all aboard and sunk our ship. There would have been no witnesses and the U.S. would have most likely blamed Egypt.

Do you really think Israel is a friend of the United States or is merely using us to further their agenda at our expense? If the U.S. nukes Iran, it will be for the benefit of Israel and the banksters rather than to protect America.

It is incomprehensible that our government continues to support Israel with billions of dollars and high tech weapons. So many of the problems in the world today are the result of our continued support of the Israeli **Zionist** government. Note that I did not say the **Jewish** government of Israel. I sometime even wonder if there are any true Jewish believers in the Israeli government. The Talmud says that the country of Israel, as prophesized in the Bible, is not to be until the coming of their messiah; which hasn't happened yet. Until such time, the Jews are to live in their host country in peace.

There are millions of Jews in the world that do not support the Zionist movement just as there are millions of Americans that don't support United States governmental policies. The same type of "False Flag" operation was probably utilized with the September 11, 2001 attacks. The nineteen hijackers were most likely **set up** to shield the true perpetrators. Some of the alleged hijackers have actually turned up alive. It makes one wonder if any of them were really on the hijacked planes. The result was that the attack helped persuade public opinion to allow Bush, Cheney, and Rumsfeld to invade Afghanistan and Iraq. Hopefully we will not fall for this horrible dishonest tactic again to justify attacking Iran.

USS Liberty Ship photo courtesy of James Ennes, author of: "Assault on the Liberty: The True Story of the Attack by Israel on an American Intelligence ship."

Religious Doctrine

Before discussing how religious doctrine is used as a form of "Control", I want to explain my own personal beliefs regarding religious matters. First, I am not a Christian. At least not a Christian as described in the Bible. I believe a true Christian follows what Jesus Christ taught, not what the apostle Paul, the Catholic Church and King Constantine added later. Second, when I tell someone I am not a Christian many times they assume that I am an atheist, which I am not. I consider myself to be a "Deist." **(Believing that God exists and created the world but thereafter assumed no control over it)** Most of the Founding Fathers were Deists who also believe that God does not directly communicate with humans, either by revelation or by sacred books. And they deny the divinity of Jesus.

The reasons why I am not a Christian as described in the Bible are: (1) I do not believe in the virgin birth of Jesus, (2) I do not believe that Jesus rose from the dead, (3) I don't believe in the Trinity, (4) I don't believe that Jesus performed any miracles and (5) I don't believe he died on the cross. This in no way should diminish the importance of the Jesus stories and the **Christ Consciousness** that resides in all of us. The positive message that has been attributed to Jesus has helped millions of people cope with their problems and has given them hope for eternal life.

I do believe in a Creator (God) and a **physical** Jesus-just not the mythical Jesus as portrayed in the Bible. I cannot explain it in any more detail. No one else can either. How do you prove something based on faith?

To see the progression of lower to higher animals, I believe that it would be naïve for anyone to think it stops with man just because we cannot perceive the next level above us. A goldfish does not understand how a carburetor works, but that does not mean an automobile doesn't exist nor does it mean there is no intelligent life above the Goldfish. Could this intelligent life above man be called "God?" I believe in the basic teachings of the historical Jesus (not the Biblical Jesus), the Ten Commandments, the Golden

Rule, Love thy Neighbor, respect of others religious beliefs, and in the importance of my attempting to enrich the lives of everyone I meet.

My religious studies have convinced me that the Jesus as described in the Bible is a myth and that the Bible is merely a collection of outright lies and exaggerations with a few historical facts sprinkled in. The biblical Jesus as portrayed in the bible is not the true Jesus. As stated earlier, the Biblical Jesus is a fantasy written by the Apostle Paul, the Catholic Church, and King Constantine. The Jesus described in the Dead Sea Scrolls and other ancient texts, who was married to Mary *Magdalene* and who most probably had children, is the real Jesus. There is no argument that there was a physical Jesus who was a great prophet, teacher and healer- but he was not "God".

Jesus was a Jew that never intended to launch a worldwide religious movement called "Christianity." Others hijacked his name and pieces of his beliefs and added their own agenda and called it "Christianity." People 2,000 years ago knew Jesus was not "God" and that his mother was not a virgin. However after the Catholic Church had millions of nonbelievers- "heretics"- killed, the mythical **Biblical** version of Jesus gradually became the accepted account.

I hesitate to share this opinion with Christians for fear of taking a belief system away from someone who derives comfort and security from it. **An alternative to their beliefs is to explain to them that there are many answers to questions that man is not even intelligent enough to ask. That doesn't mean that these answers don't exist. Somewhere in the answers to these questions, there may be something that will be in our best interest after we die.**

Could it be possible that when we were born here we died somewhere else and when we die in this existence we will be born into another dimension? Is this the means that the "Spirit" self continues to improve by experiencing life in the physical world. Possibly it is just one continuing journey of spiritual growth. This idea of reincarnation does offer a plausible explanation why idiot savants and some young children have such extraordinary memories, and abilities involving mathematics, music, speaking and understanding other languages, etc. Could their memories and abilities have been transferred from one life to another? This is only a theory but my guess should be just as good as anyone else's.

Most of the references of reincarnation have been edited out of the early translations of the bible because a belief in reincarnation would take away the necessity of one belonging to an organized "Church". Reincarnation was a prevalent belief of the people living 2,000 years ago.

There are two extremes concerning religious beliefs; the religious fanatics at one end and the atheists at the other. I find it logical, for me at least, to be somewhere in the middle. The fanatics are completely out of control using their distorted religious beliefs to justify their ungodly actions, and the atheist's at the other end don't believe there is **anything** after death. The best argument of why the Atheists don't believe in God is that the Old Testament is filled with absurdities. I think they make a good point but they don't consider that there is so much more knowledge that man can't perceive because of his limited abilities. Our senses have limitations that can only sense certain frequencies of light and sound but that doesn't mean nothing else exits beyond our present limitations. Look how mans' knowledge was expanded with the invention of the telescope and microscope. There will be much more knowledge acquired by us in the future by extending our senses even more. Does this future knowledge not exist simply because our senses at the present can't perceive it?

The Old Testament is filled with stories of death and destruction condoned or caused by the "Lord". There appears to be much more space in the Bible devoted to cruelty than the love and respect of one's fellow man. This, among other things, makes me question the divinity of the Bible.

In the appendix of this book is a list of selected Bible references that should help you determine if the Bible is divinely inspired.

People don't realize how closely "Jesus" came to not being considered God. (Trinity) The word "Trinity" doesn't even appear in the Bible. However, **The First Epistle General of John verses 7 and 8** says, "For there are three that bear record in heaven, the Father, the Word*, and the Holy Ghost: and these three are one. And there are three that bear witness in earth, the Spirit, and the water, and the blood: and these three agree in one."   *"Word" is interpreted as "Son."   Does this really explain the idea of the "Trinity?"

At the Council of Nicene in 325 AD, King Constantine kept sending home Bishops who would not vote for the "Trinity" concept. The remaining Bishops finally voted to declare Jesus as God because failure to do so would be the same as having a religion that worships a mere mortal man and that would be idol worship; the same as the Pagans' belief. Cardinal Newman, in his book, "The Development of the Christian Religion," admits that ... "Temples, incense, oil lamps, votive offerings, holy water, holidays and season of devotions, processions, blessing of fields, sacerdotal vestments, the tonsure (of priests and monks and nuns), images ... are all of pagan origin..." (Page 359).   Many other scholars believe that up to 75% of the rites and ceremonies of the Roman Catholic Church are of pagan origin.

I am sure many Christians would claim that Jesus claimed to be God in the Bible scriptures.   There are several places where biblical translators give you the **impression** that Jesus **claimed** to be God, when in fact he did not. (Ref. Mathew 26:63-64, and Luke 22:70)

Some people even believe that the Bible claims that women don't have a soul. There are many references in the Bible that would give you that impression. In fact the Bible portrays women as second class citizens and their main purpose is for the pleasure and company of men. However other ancient documents, not included in the Bible, have revealed that women were respected by the true historical Jesus and were involved in the early Christian movement.

The TV evangelists use one's fear of dying and guilt from their so called sins to control them and to encourage them to financially support their church and their lavish life styles. Governments sometimes plot to take advantage of the differences in religious beliefs to stir up animosity between religions or sects. It is no accident the Shiites and Sunnis are fighting each other and the Muslims and Jews are killing each other by the thousands. The hatred and mistrust of the various religious groups oftentimes assists our government in accomplishing its clandestine and secret agendas. This can be very profitable to the military industrial complex; **War is more profitable than peace.**

The Catholic Church's killing of millions of heretics during the Dark Ages is appalling. However, it was a pretty effective means of "Control." The Catholic Church and the Apostle Paul's additions to the original teachings of Jesus have so distorted Christianity that Jesus himself would not recognize his movement today. If Jesus returned today, I think he would say, "You people weren't listening! This is not what I taught you to do!" The Jesus movement today should be more appropriately called *"Churchianity"* or *"Paulianity"* instead of *"Christianity."*

Indebtedness

People with excessive debt are not free and are easily controlled. Our government's present monetary policies make it very difficult for the average person to ever get out of debt and virtually impossible for our government to get out of debt. Charles Collins, a banker and former presidential candidate, believes we will never get out of debt because the Federal Reserve is in control of our money. He says it is perpetuated by the Federal Reserve making us borrow the money from them, at interest, to pay the interest that's already accumulated. It's an ever expanding, never ending cycle.

We are going to have a deep depression, either in the form of a severe economic crash or continued relentless inflation. The Federal Reserve's monetary policies are creating these conditions to enrich its private stockholders; same as it did in the Great Depression of the 1930's. Remember, wealth will not be destroyed; it will merely be transferred from the poor and middle class to the wealthy. People in debt are so busy working on paying off their debt that they have little time left to get involved in politics and discovering the truth regarding how they are controlled.

Withholding Scientific Knowledge

As a form of Mind Control, "Withholding Scientific Knowledge" is an extremely difficult subject to address because of how hard it is to obtain the facts. Much of the secrecy is suppressed by our government because of military secrets which we don't want to fall into the hands of the enemy. Other secrets fall into the category of conspiracy theories like UFO's, Aliens and earth beings based on the Moon and Mars and reports of alien abductions and advanced secret technologies used by the CIA and the Pentagon. I find the stories of UFO's and alien abductions very interesting but difficult to believe. When I read what Carl Sagan had to say about this subject in his book, "*The Demon Haunted World*", I tended to discount the alien and UFO stories. He believes that the "aliens" of today may have simply replaced the ghosts, witches, elves, etc. of the past. But then I read Colonel Corso's book, "The Day After Roswell" and heard UFO researcher Bud Hopkins speak, I came to believe that maybe we **have** been visited by aliens. Why would Colonel Corso lie about seeing the bodies of aliens at Fort Riley, Kansas and say that the U.S. government did reverse engineering from captured technology of the aliens to develop "transistors" "night vision", "lasers" etc? It appears the Germans were also working on some of this advanced technology in the 1940's. Were they assisted by alien technology or were their scientist's more advanced than American scientists? We have made an extraordinary amount of progress in the last half of the 20th century. Did we do it on our own, or were we assisted by some higher intelligence? In the 1940's, I could barely dream of what was to come through the many advances in television, video recorders, computers, internet, cell phones, and space exploration. It is claimed that our government is using some of Nikola Tesla's [b.1856—d.1943] inventions to control the weather and earthquakes. The Pentagon refers to this phenomenon as "Weather Warfare." (Owning the weather) It is believed that Tesla had invented a "Mechanical Resonator" that could cause earthquakes and other disturbances. Tesla claimed that his oscillator could knock down any building and split the earth in half. Whether this story is true or not, you can be sure that the Pentagon would desperately want such a device in order to be able to have a first strike capability without the fear of a retaliatory response. Another project using Tesla's technology is "HAARP." (High Frequency Active Auroral Research Program) This large array of antennas near Gakona Alaska puts a shield around the United States to protect us from missile attack. A side effect of this machine may be to alter the climate and trigger tornadoes and hurricanes. Can we believe the HAARP web site that claims it **will not** affect the weather?

A particularly unconscionable form of mind control is when our CIA uses secret knowledge to control people to commit acts such as assassinations, sabotage and to control the minds of enemy soldiers. They use new drugs for interrogation purposes, and advanced electronics for surveillance purposes. If one has watched the movie, *"The Manchurian Candidate"* one will understand the theory behind this kind of control. The CIA claims they stopped experimenting with mind control because of its unreliability. I would guess they stopped experimenting with it because they finally perfected the process.

When Sirhan Sirhan was asked if he had shot Bobby Kennedy, he answered in a dazed state, "I guess I did. They said I did". (Or something to that effect) Much of the evidence suggests that others were involved. A woman of interest in a polka dot dress was seen in the kitchen at the time of the assassination but was never found. Could this mystery woman or someone else have fired the fatal shots? Some people have speculated that there was a gun concealed inside a camera that was used to make the actual shot. Could Sirhan Sirhan have been a part of a clandestine mind control plot to assassinate Bobby Kennedy?

The more sinister aspect of 'Mind Control" is when our government clandestinely controls the minds of its citizens in secret. (All in the name of "national security"). The greatest threat to the American citizen is that which is conducted by the CIA and Federal Health programs. The secret medical experiments the government has done on our citizens in the past is deplorable. One example is the Tuskegee, Alabama experiments where African-Americans were injected with syphilis to study the effects.

Some of the ideas presented here can't be proven and may well be just another "conspiracy theory." However in my opinion, the reasons there are so many 'Conspiracy Theories' is that there are so many conspiracies. After all, "conspiracy" simply means "a secret plan or agreement between two or more people to commit an illegal or subversive act." Even if all the details are not true it appears to me that the general premise could be true i.e.; clandestine parts of our government could be working to control the minds of thousands of its citizens without their permission. [Reference Jim Keith's book, "Mind Control/World Control"]

I would like to have seen an honest medical and psychological evaluation of Lee Harvey Oswald, Sirhan Sirhan, John Hinckley, Patti Hearst, Jim Jones, Mark David Chapman, and Timothy McVeigh to see if they had been subjected to any kind of "Mind Control." In fact, it has been reported that many of these people were under the care of top CIA doctors with expertise in Mind Control and drugs. Also it would be interesting to see if there were any links to each other in other ways. Some of these people left suspicious diaries or incriminating evidence implicating themselves, and most seem to have acted like "zombies" if they were involved in killing someone and don't remember exactly what happened.

Some of the mind control methods supposedly used today involve drugs, shock treatment, hypnosis, brain implants, microwave radiation and sensory deprivation. Some people have been subjected to sadistic and ritualistic experiences so horrible that their brain sets up individual compartments to deal with these experiences. If this defense mechanism was not implemented, they would most likely have gone insane.

The Skeptic's Dictionary by Robert Todd Carroll makes the following comments about the government and "Mind-Control":

"There also seems to be a growing belief that the U.S. government, through its military branches or agencies such as the CIA, is using a number of horrible devices aimed at disrupting the brain. Laser weapons, isotropic radiators, infrasound, non-nuclear electromagnetic pulse generators, and high-power microwave emitters have been mentioned. It is known that government agencies have experimented on humans in mind control studies with and without the knowledge of their subjects (Scheflin 1978). The claims of those who believe they have been unwilling victims of "mind control" experiments should not be dismissed as impossible or even as improbable. Given past practice and the amoral nature of our military and intelligence agencies, such experiments are not implausible. However, these experimental weapons, which are aimed at disrupting brain processes, should not be considered mind control weapons. To confuse, disorient or otherwise debilitate a person through chemicals or electronically is not to control that person. To make a person lose control of himself is not the same as gaining control over him. We can't be certain that our government is capable of controlling anyone's mind, though it is clear that many people in many governments lust after such power.

"Molestation and Mistreatment of Children and Adults

Almost daily there is something in the newspaper or on TV describing a molestation case. If a young person or an unstable adult is molested they will many times suppress the horror of what happened to them causing them to be easily controlled by the molester. We are not talking about just sexual molestation but also other evil and sadistic acts. When this happens, the mind completely blocks out or compartmentalizes the event in its brain in an attempt to maintain a degree of sanity.

Hunger

It seems like there is a concerted effort to **not** solve the "Hunger" problem facing the world today. It is easier to control a hungry population than one that is well fed. There is an abundance of food necessary to feed the world's population but the leaders do not take the necessary steps to solve this problem. Even the United Nations has been unable or **unwilling** to solve the hunger crisis. Is there a secret agenda to weed out millions of the third world's population through starvation? If so, wouldn't it be more humane to feed the hungry and at the same time embark on a program of birth control?

Drug Addiction

In the 1950's and 60's LSD was used by the CIA on unwitting subjects for the purpose of experimentation and later for control. There are cases known where politicians have been controlled by providing them with addictive and recreational drugs for political favors. Illegal drug money has been used to finance clandestine assassinations and other covert activity by our own government agencies. (Reference the book, *"Whiteout: The CIA, Drugs and the Press"* by Cockburn and St. Clair) It would be financially detrimental to many individuals and government agencies if they did not share in the drug profits to support their clandestine and illegal projects. It is not in the best interests of these people to win the "War on Drugs." When the government announces that they have arrested a drug cartel leader, what they are really saying is that they have just eliminated one of their own competitors.

Blackmail

More than anything else today, **blackmail** may be the leading force shaping media bias and the United States foreign and domestic policies. Blackmail has always been involved in politics but today it is also controlling the information or disinformation that we get from the main stream media.

How many of us have secrets that could at minimum embarrass us or at worst destroy our careers and marriage and maybe even land us in prison. What if you were a high placed government official, a top executive of a radio and TV network or editor of a large newspaper and you had been involved in drug use or distribution, a gay or lesbian affair, an affair with a mistress, laundering of money, bribes to vote for unpopular causes, bribes to fake stories about respectable people, bribes to lie under oath, etc, etc. You would be an easy target for the blackmailer.

The most likely person who would have the information to blackmail someone would be a person or company that had the ability to spy on them by monitoring their telephone conversations and internet activity. Believe it or not there is a company in the United States that does have this capability and worst of all it is a foreign owned company.

This company is owned by Israeli interests. It is called **AMDOCS** and its subsidiary is **COMVERSE INFOSYS.** Fox News did a complete story on this company's ability to monitor our phone calls but for some unknown reason it has been taken off the internet. It is believed that Comverse Infosys has equipment permanently installed into the phone system that allows instant monitoring by law enforcement agencies. Any government official or citizen that suggests that this be investigated is committing career suicide.

One needs to be alert and aware of the different kinds of "Thought Control "and "Mind Control" being perpetrated so they can minimize the chances of becoming a victim.

Population Control

Eugenics is the term used to describe the process of improving the quality of the human species by such means as discouraging reproduction of humans with genetic defects or those that have undesirable traits. There are both positive and negatives issues involving eugenics.

Over population causing worldwide hunger epidemics and the weakening of the gene pool through the reproduction of inferior people are legitimate concerns that could have long term negative consequences for the human race. The solutions to these problems is complicated from the part morality has to do with this issue. Is it moral for us to interfere with nature and conduct population control techniques in secret because it is in the long run best for the human race?

Hitler certainly thought it was. My opinion is if population control is done in secret it is wrong. Birth control and eugenics issues should be done in the light of day with the approval of the people rather than in secret as it is being done today.

Eugenics Quotes

"It does not, however, seem impossible that by an attention to breed, a certain degree of improvement, similar to that among animals, might take place among men. Whether intellect could be communicated may be a matter of doubt: but size, strength, beauty, complexion, and perhaps even longevity are in a degree transmissible... As the human race could not be improved in this way, without condemning all the bad specimens to celibacy, it is not probable, that an attention to breed should ever become general. (**Thomas R. Malthus.** *An Essay on Population.* **1798)**

In order to stabilize world population, we must eliminate 350,000 people per day. It is a horrible thing to say, but it is just as bad not to say it." (**Jacques Cousteau, 1991 UNESCO courier)**

"Society has no business to permit degenerates to reproduce their kind.... Any group of farmers, who permitted their best stock not to breed, and let all the increase come from the worst stock, would be treated as fit inmates for an asylum.... Some day we will realize that the prime duty, the inescapable duty of the good citizens of the right type is to leave his or her blood behind him in the world; and that we have no business to permit the perpetuation of citizens of the wrong type. The great problem of civilization is to secure a relative increase of the valuable as compared with the less valuable or noxious elements in the population... The problem cannot be met unless we give full consideration to the immense influence of heredity..." (**Theodore Roosevelt to Charles B. Davenport, January 3, 1913, Charles B. Davenport Papers, Department of Genetics, Cold Spring Harbor, N.Y**

"Political unification in some sort of world government will be required... Even though... any radical eugenic policy will be for many years politically and psychologically impossible, it will be important for UNESCO to see that the eugenic problem is examined with the greatest care, and that the public mind is informed of the issues at stake so that much that now is unthinkable may at least become thinkable."(**Sir Julian Huxley, UNESCO: Its Purpose and Its Philosophy**

"I do not pretend that birth control is the only way in which population can be kept from increasing... War... has hitherto been disappointing in this respect, but perhaps bacteriological war may prove more effective. If a Black Death could be spread throughout the world once in every generation survivors could procreate freely without making the world too full... The state of affairs might be somewhat unpleasant, but what of that? Really high-minded people are indifferent to happiness, especially other people's... There are three ways of securing a society that shall be stable as regards population. The first is that of birth control, the second that of infanticide or really destructive wars, and the third that of general misery except for a powerful minority..." **Bertrand Russell, *"THE IMPACT OF SCIENCE ON SOCIETY"* 1953)**

"And advanced forms of biological warfare that can "target" specific genotypes may transform biological warfare from the realm of terror to a politically useful tool."-*"The Project for a New American Century, Rebuilding America's Defenses,"* **p. 60.**

MARGARET SANGER QUOTES, Founder of the Birth Control League (which later became Planned Parenthood)

No woman shall have the legal right to bear a child... without a permit for parenthood."

The most merciful thing that a family does to one of its infant members is to kill it." We should hire three or four colored ministers, preferably with social-service backgrounds and with engaging personalities. The most successful educational approach to the Negro is through a religious appeal. We don't want the word to go out that we want to exterminate the Negro population. and the minister is the man who can straighten out that idea if it ever occurs to any of their more rebellious members."
Margaret Sanger's December 19, 1939 letter to Dr. Clarence Gamble, 255 Adams Street, Milton, Massachusetts. Original

source: Sophia Smith Collection, Smith College, North Hampton, Massachusetts. Also described in Linda Gordon's Woman's Body, Woman's Right: A Social History of Birth Control in America. New York: Grossman Publishers, 1976.

"Eugenics is ... the most adequate and thorough avenue to the solution of racial, political and social problems."

Authors note: It should be obvious that there are some very famous people with atrocious ideas about Eugenics. Apparently their intellect is clouding their judgment.

USS 'Maine entering Havana Harbor on January 25, 1898, where the ship would explode three weeks later.

February 27, 1933, the Reichstag (parliament) Building in Berlin, Germany was burned. Was it an accident?

Chapter Three
The Hegelian Dialectic
Problem—Reaction—Solution

(1) The government creates or exploits a **problem** and blames it on others.

(2) The people **react** by asking the government for help and are willing to give up their rights.

(3) The government offers the **solution** that was planned long before the crisis.

Do you suppose "The Hegelian Dialectic" is alive and well today? You are probably thinking, "I certainly hope not." Well, I am sad to say it **is** alive and well.

Georg Wilhelm Friedrich Hegel (1770-1831) was a German philosopher who wrote "Science of Logic" in 1812. Many people believe that he was one of the greatest of the German philosophers. Others believe that Hegel's views are leading us into a dictatorship against the proletariat. (The class of wage-earning workers in our society) i.e.; **assaults on individual's liberty, unnecessary wars, privacy issues, expanded police powers, land confiscation for the good of the majority, and covert actions by the CIA.** The Hegelian Dialectic is the framework being used by our government to guide people's thoughts and actions into conflicts that lead us to a predetermined solution. Karl Marx and Friedrich Engels used Hegel's theory of the dialectic to support their theory of Communism. Once one understands this principle they will begin to see how it is being utilized today in our everyday lives, much to the detriment of mankind.

Following are some examples of "The Hegelian Dialectic" that have occurred in the past:

It is believed that Emperor Nero was responsible for the fire in 64 CE that burned much of Rome. **(The Government creates or**

Exploits the problem...) To dispel the rumor that he had anything to do with it, Nero blamed it on the "Christians" who were hated because of their religious beliefs. **(The people react by asking the government for help...)** Then he savagely butchered them. **(The government offers the solution...)** It is believed by some historians that all this was done by Nero simply because he didn't have enough land to build his palace.

On April 25, 1898 the United States declared war with Spain following the sinking of the Battleship Maine in Havana harbor on February 15, 1898.   Had the ship sunk because of sabotage from Spain or was it sunk from natural causes or could the U.S. have blown up its own ship? Contrary to the opinions of technical experts, our government blamed Spain for the explosion. **(The government creates or exploits a problem...)** Public opinion now supported the government's unjust declaration of war with Spain. **(The government offers the solution...)**

On the night of February 27, 1933, the Reichstag (parliament) Building in Berlin, Germany was burned.   Was it caused by accident, was it sabotaged by foreigners, or was it a deliberately set fire by the newly established government? **(The government creates or exploits a problem...)** Hitler then declared himself Furor and declared Martial Law and suspended all basic human rights. The burning of the parliament building effectively turned public opinion against the Nazi opponents. The day after the fire, Hitler's dictatorship began with the enactment of a decree which suspended all constitutional protection of political, personal, and property rights. This was all done for "The protection of the people." **(The people react by asking the government for help...)**

 These examples sounds a lot like what the United States did in enacting The Patriot Act in 2001 only one month after the 9-11 attacks. **One might logically assume that the act was written in anticipation of the attack!**

In 1962 the United States government wanted to create a pretext for war with Cuba and oust the communist leader Fidel Castro. To accomplish this goal and to change U.S. public opinion, the "Northwoods" document was created by the Joint Chiefs of Staff. This document included a plan to commit a series of terrorist acts against America and blame them on the Cuban government. (False Flag Operation) **(The government creates or exploits a problem…)** Apparently Secretary of Defense, Robert McNamara, would not approve of such a horrible plan to kill innocent people and commit acts of terrorism on our own people.

On May 1, 2001, the ABC News web site did a book review by David Ruppe entitled, **U.S. Military Drafted Plans to Terrorize U.S. Cities to Provoke War With Cuba.** The article is as follows:

"In the early 1960's, America's top military leaders reportedly drafted plans to kill innocent people and commit acts of terrorism in U.S. cities to create public support for a war against Cuba. Code named operation 'Northwoods', the plans reportedly included the possible assassination of Cuban émigrés, sinking boats of Cuban refugees on the high seas, hijacking planes, blowing up a U. S. ship, and even orchestrating violent terrorism in U.S. cities.

The plans were developed as ways to trick the American public and the international community into supporting war to oust Cuba's then new leader, communist Fidel Castro.

America's top military brass even contemplated causing U.S. military casualties, writing: 'We could blow up a U.S. ship in Guantanamo Bay and blame Cuba,' and, 'casualty lists in U.S. newspapers would cause a helpful wave of national indignation.'

Details of the plans are described in "Body of Secret's" (Doubleday), a new book by investigative reporter James Bamford about the history of America's largest spy agency, the National Security Agency. However the plans were not connected to the agency, he notes. The plans had the written approval of all the Joint Chiefs of Staff and were presented to President Kennedy's defense secretary, Robert McNamara, in March, 1962. But they apparently were rejected by the civilian leadership and have gone undisclosed for nearly 40 years.

'These were Joint Chiefs of Staff documents. The reason these were held secret for so long is the Joint Chiefs never wanted to give these up because they were so embarrassing,' Bamford told ABCNews.com

'The whole point of a democracy is to have leaders responding to the public will, and here this is the complete reverse, the military trying to trick the American people into a war that they want but that nobody else wants.'....

The documents show the 'Joint Chiefs of Staff drew up and approved plans for what may be the most corrupt plan ever created by the U.S. government,' writes Bamford.

For those readers who didn't believe that our elected leaders could be so evil as to even consider such a plan, you might want to take another look at the 9-11 cover up.

The bombing of the World Trade Center in 1993, the bombing of the Alfred P. Murrah Federal Building in Oklahoma City on April 19, 1995 and the September 11, 2001 attacks may well be other examples of "The **Problem, Reaction, Solution** method".

There are several excellent documentaries that raise enough unanswered questions to make one believe that our government was most likely involved or had prior knowledge as what was to take place in all three of these incidences. Even if our government wasn't involved, which I doubt, public opinion was altered over night. The attack on the World Trade Center in 1993 wasn't enough to change public opinion to wage war in the Middle East but the September 11th attacks certainly were. The plans for war in the Middle East were probably planned prior to these events. (See the neocons own web site- Project for a New American Century) President Bush had launch orders on his desk and troops near the border of Afghanistan two days before 9-11, ready to attack.

Chapter Four
9-11 Attack on the World Trade Center
Another Pearl Harbor

Prior to Japan's attack on the United States naval base at Pearl Harbor on Sunday morning, December 7, 1941, the American people were not willing to go to war in Europe. After all, WWI had been the war to end all wars. The attack on Pearl Harbor pushed the public's opinion from isolationism to an all-out acceptance of the war.

The "surprise" attack completely destroyed 188 aircraft and approximately 2400 American service men lost their lives with 1,178 more being wounded. Two destroyers were damaged beyond repair, two US Naval Battleships were a total loss and one mine layer was heavily damaged.

The next day, December 8, 1941, President Franklin Delano Roosevelt addressed Congress requesting a Declaration of War with Japan. The Senate and House of Representatives approved of the war declaration unanimously with the sole exception of one vote. President Roosevelt made this now famous quote, "A date which will live in infamy." Another famous quote was supposedly made by Japan's Admiral Yamamoto, "I fear all we have done is to awaken a sleeping giant and fill him with a terrible resolve." Apparently no one has been able to prove that the Admiral actually said this but as a child in the 1950's, I remember hearing this same quote. Japan justified its invasion of Manchuria, French Indo China and the Pacific Islands as mere "colonization"- the same as what Great Britain and the United States had done earlier.

There is evidence that shows Roosevelt provoked the Japanese and that he knew of the impending attack and allowed it to happen in order that public opinion would accept the United States going to war with Japan. Sound familiar! Now let's fast forward to the 9-11, 2001 attack on the World Trade Center in New York City.

I am sure everyone old enough to remember that fateful morning recalls the terror and misbelief of what happened. I had gotten up early that morning and had just turned the TV news on when the first plane hit one of the towers. Quickly I called to my wife to get up to see what was happening. We, the same as most people around the world, spent nearly the entire day glued to the TV. As the story unfolded over the next few days, I had more and more questions as to what really happened. Information that was being broadcast by the controlled media didn't seem to adequately answer my questions. As the months and years passed I became even more skeptical of the government's version of what happened and who was involved. How could 19 Arab hijackers have actually taken over these planes using box cutters and done this much damage to our country? If you believe that our government was **not** involved in any way and believe that those that **do believe** that our government was involved or had prior knowledge of the attack are "Conspiracy Nuts", then you have simply not studied the facts enough. If you have never heard of the term, "Thermite" or don't know that building Seven collapsed without being hit by a plane then it is obvious you are not qualified to pass judgment on the so called "Conspiracy Theorists." View the documentary movies like "Loose Change Final Cut" and "9-11 Ripple Effect." After viewing these documentaries, you may change your mind as to what really happened.

There are two basic theories put forth by the "Conspiracy Theorists;" (1) individuals in our government knew of the impending attacks and intentionally failed to act or (2) high level rogue elements in the US government performed a "false flag" operation intending to blame the attacks on Arab terrorists so as to alter public opinion and give us an excuse to attack Afghanistan and Iraq. This would also facilitate increased military spending and allow our government to reduce domestic civil rights. All of this would greatly enhance Israel's position in the Middle East. The Patriot Act was passed only one month after the attack. There are many other excellent theories voiced by the "9-11 Truth Movement."

Government's Account

The government's account stated that 19 Arab terrorists hijacked four commercial airplanes by using knives, box cutters, pepper spray, and fake explosives. At 8:46 AM and 9:03 AM flights 11 and 175 crashed into the twin towers of the World Trade Center causing them to collapse soon after- words. Building Seven also collapsed the same day from fires started by debris from the collapse of the North Tower. American Airlines Flight 77 crashed at 9:37 AM into the Pentagon and flight 93 crashed in an open field in Pennsylvania at 10:03 AM after the passengers stormed the cockpit.

Our government was able to identify all the hijackers with names and photographs the very next day after the attack. They were able to link them to the terrorist organization al-Qaeda, headed by Osama Bin Laden who later claimed responsibility for the attacks. *(Note: Experts have said that the video tape of Osama Bin Laden claiming responsibility for the attack is a fake)*

Government's Sources

- The reports from government investigators.
- 9-11 Commission Report (More appropriately the 9-11 Omission Report)
- Federal Emergency Management Agency (FEMA) studied building performances.
- National Institute of Standards and Technology (NIST)

Investigations by Non-Government Sources That Support the Governments Account

- National Fire Protection Association
- Purdue University and Northwest University
- Articles supporting these facts and theories appearing in magazines such as Popular Mechanics, Scientific American and Time.

It is difficult to believe the government's account as to what happened on 9-11. Following are some of the many questions that have not been adequately explained or covered by the government.

(1) One would think that the pilots flying in the four hijacked airliners would have taken some type of evasive actions such as cabin decompression or rolling the planes over when they discovered that the plane had been taken over and passengers were being killed. Weren't there any military passengers, retired police officers, etc or other able bodied passengers that could have resisted someone with a knife or box cutters in their hands? It has been reported that Todd Beamer was the passenger that led the now famous passenger revolt on Flight 93, by uttering the words, "Lets Roll." The only problem is that there were several other passengers that would have been more likely to have taken on this job. Reportedly there was on board Jeremy Glick, a former national judo champion, Mark Bingham, a former champion rugby player, Tom Burnett, a former college football quarterback, Louis Nacke 200 pound weight lifter, Cee Cee Lyles, a former police detective, Richard Guadagno an enforcement officer who had received training in hand to hand combat and William Cashman, a former paratrooper with the 101st Airborne. It is unbelievable to me that the Arab hijackers armed with box cutters were just too much for these passengers. If, as we were told, flight 93 (the plane that crashed in Pennsylvania) did have passengers that resisted, why was there no resistance on the other three?

(2) Why did it take our government almost a year and a half to initiate an independent investigation into the worst case of domestic terrorism ever made against the United States?

(3) With a huge budget of thirty billion dollars a year, why were the CIA, FBI and the other intelligence agencies caught completely unaware of the attack and yet 24 hours later had pictures and files on the alleged 19 hijackers.

(4) On the morning of the terror attacks, the original reports were saying that **five** planes were unaccounted for. Later the Federal

authorities revised the number to four planes without giving an adequate explanation.

(5) Prior to the attack, these transcontinental flights were heavily booked. However on 9-11 only 266 passengers were on flights that would normally carry as many as 1,328 passengers. Why were they only booked at 20% of their capacity?

(6) Why weren't fighter jets sent to intercept the four hijacked airliners as soon as it was obvious they had been hijacked? Wouldn't it be an extremely odd coincidence that a similar training exercise was going on at the same time with a scenario closely approximating the real attack?

(7) Why would the government refuse to release and keep secret the copies of the recorded transcripts made between the air traffic controllers and the hijacked planes?

(8) The grainy, inaudible video tapes that supposedly proved that Osama bin Laden was linked to the attacks were adamantly dismissed by translators because they disagreed on the Arabic translation. How can our government continue to insist Osama bin Laden was linked to the attacks when he repeatedly denied that he had anything to do with it.

(9) How can the reports of explosions coming from the basement and upper floors of the Twin Towers, witnessed by many people including firemen, be dismissed especially when the buildings' collapses appeared to be exactly like a controlled demolition?

(10) Other planes have hit buildings in other parts of the world resulting in fire but no building collapse. What made the difference in this case to cause the collapses?

(11) Why was debris at the World Trade Center removed before the evidence could be properly examined?

(12) It would be interesting to see a list of employees who did not show up for work that day at the World Trade Center and a list of those people who profited from selling their airline stock just a few days before the attack.

(13) How do you explain that at least 6 of the suicide hijackers have been reported to still be alive?

(14) What connection, if any, is there between the spy network of Israeli "art students" that were operating throughout the U.S. in close proximity to where the hijackers were purported to be living?

(15) What caused the collapse of the nearby WTC Buildings 6 and 7 when they weren't even hit by a plane?

(16) Was key evidence planted to implicate Arabs in the attack? How could Arab flight training manuals and religious material be found at Boston's Logan airport and a passport of one of the alleged hijackers be found in the WTC rubble. The odds are pretty high that this would not have happened. And, how could a paper passport survive the high temperatures and fire at ground zero?

(17) Why haven't we received a full explanation of the five Israelis seen cheering and photographing the collapse of the Twin Towers.

(18) Have the investigators looked into the technology that allows the remote control of a military "Global Hawk" which is the approximate size of a Boeing 737? Since it is a well-known fact that none of the hijackers were accomplished pilots or navigators, this scenario should warrant further investigation.

(19) Why does the U.S. media and government authorities continue to ignore the business relationship between the Bush family and the Bin Laden Group?

(20) Why did the United States military have war plans to invade Afghanistan several months **before** the 9-11 attack on the World Trade Center and the Pentagon?

(21) How do you explain the two huge spikes in the seismic record on 9-11 that were recorded prior to the collapse? Wouldn't this be proof of a huge explosion that could have been instrumental in bringing down the Twin Towers?

(22) Remember the old adage that says to solve a crime, just follow the money? Just ask yourself, "Who profits"? The Muslim fanatics profited by bragging that they could inflict enormous damage to the United States which in turn gave them a great deal of prestige and the ability to recruit even more terrorists to their cause. But by far, the groups that profited the most were the neo-cons in our government, the Israelis and the American Zionists. This does not **prove** who was responsible but should certainly warrant further investigation into the possibilities of Israel being involved.

The government's version of what happened on 9-11 is the most farfetched conspiracy theory of all. It is amazing to me that the public actually believes that 19 Arab hijackers controlled by a man in a cave half way across the world, armed only with box cutters and without the skills to fly even a small Cessna type airplane, were able to hijack four commercial airliners, and crash two of them into the World Trade Center and one into the Pentagon.

I have recently been examining all the known superstitions of the world, and do not find in our particular superstition (Christianity) one redeeming feature. They are all alike, founded on fables and mythology.
<u>Thomas Jefferson</u>

All national institutions of churches, whether Jewish, Christian or Turkish, appear to me no other than human inventions, set up to terrify and enslave mankind, and monopolize power and profit.
<u>Thomas Paine</u>

Chapter Five
Religious Beliefs

I was brought up in the Presbyterian Church in St. Joseph, Missouri, but early on found myself unable to believe all that I was told about God and Jesus. I sincerely regret that when I was about 21 years of age, I shared my beliefs with my mother who was a devout Christian. I am sure she was very disappointed that her son was not a Christian and probably blamed herself for not getting me more involved in her church.

Is The Bible Divinely Inspired?

I have read many books about religion and have attended several different church denominations in an attempt to discover the truth regarding Christianity. As a favor to a close friend in 1968, I attended a "Revival" at a Southern Baptist Church in Bartlesville, Oklahoma. I remember the pastor telling a joke about a Negro man that didn't know the difference between a "Chandelier" and a "Cadillac." Not only did I not get the joke, I couldn't believe that this pastor would say something so degrading to the Negro race. Several years later, I attended the Church of one of my relatives in St. Joseph, Mo. and one of the white deacons, that heavily supported the church, was threatening to leave the church because a young black boy was about to join the church sponsored Cub Scout group. Again, I could not believe that someone that professed to be a Christian would have this negative attitude toward a young Negro boy that only wanted to be a cub scout. It would be interesting to know what effect this had on this young Negro boy after he became an adult.

As a young man in the 1960's, I began to share my views concerning "integration" with my friends and relatives. Over and over good Christian church goers would say, "I agree that Negro's should have equal rights but I think they are moving a little too fast." I would reply, "Let's see------, they were freed from slavery in the 1860's and it is now 1960, one hundred years doesn't seem too fast to me!" It was difficult for me to understand why our government had to pass Civil Rights Legislation when we had so many religious people in this country who could have solved the problem easily with no additional laws. The God fearing Christian people failed to act in a Christian way. Some would rationalize that they wouldn't mind having Negroes move into their neighborhood but could not take a chance on having their property values go down. I reasoned that it was a worthwhile chance to take considering the importance of the moral issue. I am quite sure that these religious experiences in my youth had a great deal to do with how I feel today about religious organizations.

After reading the Bible twice and using a yellow highlighter to mark those passages that I didn't agree with or understand, I decided that (1) the Bible was definitely not divinely inspired and (2) if I were a Christian, the Old Testament would be an embarrassment to my religion. How could the Bible be divinely inspired when it says that gays and lesbians should be put to death and women should not speak in public? What about requesting God to stop the sun so the battle of Jericho could continue? Didn't God know that the earth rotates on its axis and revolves around the sun? The Roman Catholics, a few years ago, finally apologized to Galileo for what the Church had believed were his heretic views.

These and numerous other discrepancies make it impossible for me to believe that the Bible is divinely inspired. The Bible is more likely written by prejudiced power hungry men attempting to control the ignorant masses through fear, intolerance, withholding the truth and giving themselves dominion over females.

The Catholic Church has done an excellent job in discrediting the Pagans of their religious beliefs. The irony of it is that "Christianity" is really just "Paganism" revised (especially in the Catholic Church). The twelve signs of the Zodiac became the twelve disciples in the Christian Church and the birth of a mythical Jesus corresponds to the movement of the sun as recorded on the sun dial. (the Sun of God) Up to December 22nd the sun keeps moving. Then for three days, December 22nd, 23rd, and 24th, the sun stays in the same position. When it hadn't moved, the early Christians assumed the sun was dead. On the 25th the sun started moving again in the opposite direction one degree, therefore it was thought that the Sun must be alive again (rebirth). Now we know that the **Son** Jesus was born on the 25th of December after the sun having been dead for three days. Do you really think that this analogy relates to the birth of a physical person, Jesus, or could it have possibly meant to be ascribed to a mythical Jesus? Do you see how the **Sun** became **Son**?

The "Holy Bible" was translated from the Latin "Helio Biblio" which literally means Book of the Sun.

There are numerous other explanations of religious events that correspond with various astrological events. Prior to Christianity, the Pagans recognized female gods and even accepted women into the Church; unlike the Catholics who exclude women from the higher positions of the Church. I highly recommend the documentary, "Zeitgeist" which further explains the connection of religious doctrine to astronomical events. Christianity is simply, "personification" of the astronomical stories, done to teach and control the masses.

When you consider all that the Catholic Church has done concerning child molesting, lying about the origins of Christianity, persecuting heretics, triggering religious wars, etc, I question why anyone would be a Catholic **or** a Biblical Christian after studying the available facts. In 1962, the Vatican issued a secret document called **"Crimen Sollicitationis"** Latin for **"Crime of Soliciting"** which critics say was used to silence child abuse victims. This document was enforced for 20 years by Cardinal Ratzinger before becoming Pope Benedict XVI. A true Christian is one that follows the original teachings of the <u>historical Christ</u> rather than the <u>mythical"Biblical Christ</u>."

The following outrageous statement should infuriate non Christians: Pope Eugene IV at the Council of Florence, 1441, "The Holy Roman Church firmly believes, professes and preaches that all those who are outside the Catholic Church, not only pagans but also Jews or heretics and schismatic's, cannot share in eternal life and will go into the everlasting fire which was prepared for the devil and his angels, unless they are joined to the Church before the end of their lives…" (Also reference Mathew 25:41) When I was growing up in the 1950's, I remember people saying that if you don't accept Jesus Christ as your Lord and Savior, you will go to hell!

I do not mean to criticize only the Christian religion. The Jews and Muslim faiths have just as many lies, distortions and superstitions in their "Holy Books" and belief systems. Even though I am critical of these **religions,** I very much respect many of those **people** as individuals. It is just the foundation of their religion with which I do not agree.

I find it very strange and suspicious that someone as important as the Biblical Jesus is mentioned only in the Bible and not in any of the numerous old books of Roman history. If a man 2,000 years ago could walk on water, change water into wine, bring people back from the dead, feed thousands of people from one loaf of bread and one fish, make the blind see, etc., surely he would be written about in the history of Rome, have coins with his likeness on them, paintings of himself, numerous writings attributed to him etc. His picture might even be carved on the pyramids in Egypt! Since these things didn't happen, I question even the existence of the "Biblical" Jesus. There are those who would argue that Jesus was mentioned one time by the historian Josephus. The only problem is that most historians believe that the part about Jesus is fraudulent since the writing style changes when Jesus is discussed.

You can study religion from a **faith** viewpoint or as a **scholar** but I guarantee that if you study religion based on the scholarly approach you will not come to the same conclusions as those studying it based on faith who attempt to prove their beliefs by quoting Bible passages. It means absolutely nothing to me when someone tries to prove their point by quoting the Bible. It is impossible to discuss biblical issues with someone whose argument is based on **faith**. One might as well not even try. The one that "appears" to win simply knows his Bible facts better than his opponent!

Probably 2,000 years from now people will be arguing where Harry Potter was born and if he could really fly! He must have been a real person since nowhere in the book does it say that it is fiction. They will probably explain that you just have to have **faith** that Harry Potter was a real person.

It is a great liberating feeling for me personally to be finally free from the many bogus religious beliefs and dogmas. It is one less form of control over my life. If the entire world could understand that most of their religious beliefs were mainly superstitions and mythology, we wouldn't need to continuously have wars and kill our fellow man just because they don't believe like we do.

Even though I have lost religion, "Churchianity," I have discovered "Spirituality." I believe that each one of us is composed of three separate entities; the physical, mental and spiritual self. Think of these as legs of a tripod. All three must be kept in balance or you are liable to fall. We were put on this earth to experience life and grow spiritually, so it is extremely important for our present well-being as well as our future well-being to keep these three entities in balance. This is accomplished by a proper diet and exercise, development of a positive mental attitude and recognizing the importance of positive growth within the spiritual self.

I am not an atheist but can certainly understand why they believe the way they do. I believe in the Bible verse that says, "The more you give, the more you receive." I have proven many times in my life that this particular verse is true. Most people don't realize that the reverse is also true. "The more you **take** the more you **lose**." Have you ever seen a happy thief, rapist, or murderer? The fear of getting caught and suffering the consequences is quite a burden to bear. You create your own hell right here on Earth. You don't need to die to go to Hell.

Several years ago I had a poor man, his wife and three children come into my store in Bakersfield, California and ask very timidly if I could spare some money for food for his family. He explained that they had not eaten in two days. I was busy and told him that I couldn't help because I had too many requests like this every day and simply couldn't honor them all. As they slowly walked away looking extremely depressed and hungry, I thought that this just is not right. I felt so guilty not helping them. They were believable and I felt they truly needed some help. So, I followed them outside and took them to the 7-11 convenience store across the street and bought them milk, bread, lunchmeat and some other groceries. They were very grateful and said "God bless you" in broken English and continued slowly walking down the street. I hadn't noticed during this busy Saturday but at the end of the day when I totaled up my sales for the day, I had sold over $5,000 worth of antiques and furniture. That was considered a good day for me because I normally only sold around $2,000 on Saturday. I paused and thought, "You don't suppose that it had anything to do with me helping that poor family?" The Bible does say that "The more you give, the more you receive."

A few years ago, a young man came into my store to sell an old radio because he was desperately in need of money. He said I could have the radio for $50.00 but it was so dirty and greasy, I could not readily determine its value. Feeling somewhat sorry for him, I made an offer of $25.00. He looked disappointed but under the circumstances he said, "OK." Later in the day, as I was cleaning all the dirt and grime off the radio, I discovered it was a red Bakelite radio which was fairly rare. One phone call to a collector and it was sold for $600.00. I felt very good about the profit but felt awful for not paying him his asking price of $50.00. If I would have paid what he had asked everything would have been fine. I like to make a profit but I felt that I had taken advantage of him by not paying him what he asked.

About two months later the same man came in again and this time wanted to sell me a "Jack in the Box" toy for $50.00. I didn't really want the toy because I felt that it was worth only about $5.00. Remembering how badly I felt about the first transaction, I said, "Sure $50.00 is fine." At last my conscience was clear. I gave it to one of my employees to price and she said, "What did you pay for this?" I said, "$50.00." She said, this is a rare Jack in the Box and is worth at least $150.00." I had done it again! How would I ever get even with this man? About nine months later he came into the store again and explained that his mother had kicked him out of the house and he had a job prospect but didn't have a place to get cleaned up for the interview. I said, "Come with me."

I took him to a motel and paid for his room and gave him some extra money for food. He was so happy that I had volunteered to help him and thanked me several times. Little did he know my true motives? At last my conscience was clear. It is amazing that anytime one tries to do the right thing by giving money or your time to someone in need, you seem to be rewarded in some way. Once again I had proved, at least to myself, that the more you give, the more you receive. The Bible passage is absolutely correct. These examples may just have been a coincidence but I have had the opportunity to experience many similar coincidences during the last fifty to sixty years.

Power of Prayer

I believe in the power of prayer, but you need to know how to use it effectively. Most people sit in church reciting the Lords Prayer while thinking what they will have for Sunday dinner. This is not a very effective way to pray. First you need to know the difference between prayer and meditation. A close friend of mine explained the difference to me in 1978 at an A.R.E meeting. (Association of Research and Enlightenment). She said that prayer is when you talk to God and meditation is when you listen. I thought, "Wow, what a great concept and understanding of the process of praying." I have heard that discovering examples of this kind of wisdom are referred to as one of the "Ah Hah's" in life. This was definitely one of the best "Ah Hah's" in my life. These don't come about very often so when they do you need to pause and realize how this one simple concept can change your life.

I have found that most people go through life without learning this simple important principle. They pray but don't listen. They have gotten only half of it right. I think most people believe that prayer only works when you accept Jesus Christ as your Lord and savior. That is not true. Prayer works for people of all faiths- even the atheist. Prayer is a natural law like gravity- gravity works even if you don't believe in it.

I got a chance to test this new concept twice shortly after I had received this revelation about prayer. I went to the doctor for a checkup and the doctor discovered that I had developed a hernia. He told me to come back in two weeks for another exam and he would set up an appointment at the hospital for the operation. Since I had never been operated on before, I was terrified. I immediately started a personal prayer session to see if I could heal myself using the techniques of both prayer and meditation. When I returned to the doctor two weeks later he had a puzzled look on his face. I said. "What's wrong?" He said he could barely feel the hernia and felt like it was not bad enough to operate on. He said he had never heard of a hernia healing itself. I just smiled and said, "thank you", and left. It has been over 30 years and I still have not had a hernia operation. Was it due to my prayer or did he misdiagnose the problem the first time? It really doesn't matter to me; the important thing was that I did not need to have the operation.

While in my twenties I started experiencing severe back pain. At times I was unable to walk for several days at a time. After being thoroughly examined, I was diagnosed with a degenerative disc. My doctor, in Santa Barbara, California said that there was an 80% chance of solving my back problem if he operated on it. I asked him if this were his back, what would he do? After pausing a few seconds, he said, "I would probably live with it." I went home and decided that I would attempt to use prayer to alleviate by back pain. After a week of prayer and meditation I began to lie in a tub of hot water each day and twist my body in such a way that I could crack my back like someone cracking their knuckles. I also lost some weight and starting taking calcium tablets. About 40 years passed before I finally had to have a back operation. I assume that I still had the same ruptured disk but my body had adjusted just enough that I didn't need the operation until I was seventy years old.

Steps to More Effective Prayer

I have developed a prayer procedure that has worked well for me but each person needs to develop their own method. You may want to incorporate some of my ideas to be more effective. The first thing to do is pick a proper time and place to pray (Talk to God) and meditate (Listen to God). I chose the early morning hours before any other family members were up and when I was the most alert. It is important that it be very quiet so you can keep your mind in the spiritual state. Then I chose a living room chair that I rarely sat in. In other words, don't pray in the bed room where you sleep or the kitchen where you eat or the recliner where you watch TV.

I allowed a 15 minute time limit for my prayer and mediation session. The beating of your heart is the only clock you need to advise you when the time is up. Sit upright in the chair, feet flat on the floor, with your hands in your lap, palms facing up in the receiving position.

The first five minutes should be in preparation of the mental state needed, and then you make an affirmation as to what you wish to make happen in your life. The next ten minutes is when you listen or meditate. You need to go from your existing physical state of mind to the alpha region of your brain wave pattern where you will be closer to your spiritual self and therefore more likely to understand what steps are needed to realize your prayer request. Don't expect that someone at 5:00 PM tomorrow will meet you at the corner of Hollywood and Vine and give you $100,000, or that you will be miraculously cured of some disease. It doesn't work that way. During your meditation state you will be guided in the direction for you to take to make your prayer request a reality. It is necessary for you to take some type of action to have your prayer answered.

To prepare yourself to enter the spiritual self of your being, close your eyes in a darkened room and count backwards from 100 to 1. Then recite the Lords Prayer and protect yourself by stating that you will not accept anything into your being that is not "God-like" or "Christ-like." Visualize yourself floating in darkness with a white light surrounding you for protection from any possible evil sources. This state of consciousness can make you vulnerable to both positive and negative influences. Then I make an affirmation such as- I need to heal a physical problem within my body, stop drinking or smoking, lose weight, or I need to be kinder and more understanding to my spouse, etc. My prayers have always been answered because I also make the statement that if this request is not granted then give me the strength to accept that decision. There may be a lesson for me to learn or something that as a human being I am unable to understand at this time regarding my overall spiritual growth.

I make the statement that I will pray for the same thing for the next five days. If one doesn't do this and continues to pray for the same thing day after day, you are subconsciously acknowledging that you know that your prayer will not be answered because you will be praying for the same thing tomorrow.

When it is time to listen (meditate), I convert my thought process from words to **feelings** to become more spiritual. When you think in words instead of feelings you remain in the mental state of mind instead of going to the spiritual state of mind. For best results you want to meditate when you are in the area closest to your spiritual state. To accomplish this, I think of the time I was in the beautiful redwood forest in California and saw a raccoon and her babies run across the deck of our cabin. Then I noticed a deer in the meadow and could remember smelling the pine trees and feeling the warm sun on my body and at the same time feeling the cool mountain breeze. The mountain stream running beside our cabin made a very soothing sound that I can still remember. It was one of the most beautiful places I had ever been. All of this is thinking only in feelings and no words. If you start thinking in words you are transported from your spiritual state back to your mental self.

If you have trouble believing that prayer actually works, consider that our Creator designed our bodies to be self healing. When we get cut the wound bleeds and a scab is formed. The healing process has begun. Many times the healing process consists of changing our diet and exercise regimen. Not so well understood is how the mind assists us in the healing process. Allowing the mind to assist in the healing process through prayer can be very effective if it is properly done. A part of your healing process may involve finding the right doctor and following his professional advice.

People with "Near Death Experiences" actually get the opportunity to get a glimpse of the spirit world. Through the trauma they experience, most all the stimuli they normally get from their seeing, feeling and hearing is shut down. All the physical "static" or interference to the brain has been removed and what is left is the spiritual self.

Just think what the world would be like if everyone converted from the superstitions and mythology of the Christian, Islamic, and Jewish traditions to my idea of religion. What would our world be like today if all the false religious dogmas had been given up two thousand years ago? What if people followed the original teachings of Jesus instead of what was added by the Apostle Paul, the Catholic Church and King Constantine?

Over the last few years I have been taking notes on those beliefs that bother me the most about Christianity, Islam, and Judaism. Following are some of my observations.

Christian Beliefs

The holy book of the Christians is the Bible, which we are told is "divinely inspired." It is amazing to read some of the things that the Bible actually states. You can verify the following quotations yourself in the "King James" version.

Exodus 21:15, Leviticus 20:9, Deuteronomy 21:18-21, Mark 7:9-13 and Mathew 15:4-7 *If children are shameless enough to talk back to us, we should kill them.* I surely don't believe that and I doubt any Christians believe it! It might be best to exclude this passage from your child's bible school studies.

The entire world now considers slavery as immoral and unjust. In the Bible you will find that the creator of the Universe clearly expects us to keep slaves. Leviticus 25:44-46.

The Bible even says that a man can sell his daughter into sexual slavery. (Exodus 21:7- 11) Do you think that there are any Christians today that really believe this? If a man discovers, on his wedding night, that his bride is not a virgin, he must stone her to death on her father's doorstep. (Deuteronomy 22:13-21) A good Christian will say, "Well that is in the Old Testament, The New Testament is what I rely on for my inspiration." They should read in the New Testament Mathew: 5:18-19 where Jesus endorses the entirety of the Old Testament.

For additional Bible quotes, reference the biblical quotes in the "Appendix" and then decide for yourself if the Bible is indeed "divinely inspired".

The fact that the Catholic Church has sheltered child molesters for years and has killed millions of "Heretics" should be enough to mark the end of Catholicism or at least to completely reform it by eliminating the position of Pope and the Jesuits. The Jesuits were disbanded in 1773 by Pope Clement XIV and for this he was killed by poisoning. It was 41 years before the Jesuits were once again accepted in the Catholic Church. If the information about the Black Pope being the head of the Jesuits and the Catholic Church is true, the Vatican is similar to the U.S. Government. Our so called leaders, the pope and our president, are just figure heads being manipulated by others. The "Black Pope" is the "controller" of the Catholic Church and the elite bankers in America control our president.

Many Christians believe that the entire Christian world must support the Jews in their quest to occupy the Holy Land because the Torah and the Bible in Deuteronomy 7:6 says that the Jews are Gods chosen people. Most Christians **actually believe this**! This ridiculous idea alone has cost millions of lives and untold suffering. If a person finds that belief in their religion gives comfort and strength to get through life, then I certainly don't find anything wrong with that. But to use scriptures from the various so called holy books to justify the current killings and confiscation of land in the Middle East is completely insane. The Jews are not any more Gods "chosen people" than anyone else who follows the teachings of Moses. In addition, Genesis 15:18 says that Egypt, Jordan, Saudi Arabia, Lebanon, Syria, Yemen, and part of Iraq belong to the Jews only...Now you can understand the long term expansionist's goals of the Zionists Jews.

Until Jews, Christians and Muslims accept the fact that their Holy Books are not divinely inspired, we will continue to have wars in the Middle East. Now that Israel has nuclear weapons, there is even more danger of having a war that could destroy all mankind. When one looks at the Bible, Talmud, and Koran in this light it seems to become more important than ever to understand that these books were **not** written by God or God- inspired.

Islam--Muslim Beliefs

It is difficult to respect the Muslims because of some of their religious beliefs and ties to terrorism. Their holy book, the "Koran" does not respect the lives and beliefs of other religions which make it difficult for Westerners to separate the "terrorists" from the moderate Muslims. We are continually told by our leaders that not all Muslims are bad; only the extremists! The problem is that you rarely hear any of the moderate Muslims denouncing the actions of the terrorists. I suppose they are just as afraid of them as the non-Muslims. Following are some passages from the Muslims Holy Book, the Koran:

Commands to Kill Infidels. Allah is an enemy to unbelievers – Sura 2:161

Slay them wherever ye find them and drive them out of the places whence they drove you out, for persecution is worse than slaughter. – 2:191

You must not think that those who were slain in the cause of Allah are dead. They are alive and well provided for by their Lord. – Surah 3:169-71

O believers, take not Jews and Christians as friends; they are friends of each other. Those of you who make them his friends is one of them. God does not guide an unjust people-5:54

O Prophet! Make war on the unbelievers and the hypocrites. Be harsh with them. Their ultimate abode is Hell, a hapless journey's end.- 9:111

Unbelievers are enemies of Allah and they will roast in Hell. - 41:14

Muslims are harsh against the unbelievers, merciful to one another- 48:25
Source http:www.newwave.net/-haught/Koran.html

Note: Until beliefs like these are changed, it is unlikely that there will ever be peace in the Middle East. The rest of the world should be very careful in allowing "extremist" Muslims to immigrate to their country. However, it is probably too late. The Muslims are immigrating to Europe in huge numbers and most don't assimilate into the local culture. The United States is experiencing the same problem. Most immigrants to America in the 1800's did assimilate into "Americans." But today our government supports programs that discourage them from assimilation. Many immigrants are slow to learn our language and to adopt the American culture.

In 1967 the Palestinians were granted the West Bank and Gaza strip in Israel as a Palestinian homeland. Ever since, Israel has denied them any freedom on this land. The Israelis are settling on Palestinian Arab lands in an attempt to drive them out and claim the land for themselves. The U.S. continues to support Israel politically and financially with billions of dollars of aid each year. It is time for the U.S. to stop this support and to no longer allow the Zionists in Israel and America to dictate our foreign policy in the Middle East. There are many Jews who don't support the Zionist government of Israel but seldom do you hear anything in the controlled main stream press on this issue.

It is ironic however to claim that the Palestinians should even have a Palestinian state! They already have one from the Ottoman Empire being broken up after WWl. It is called Jordan. When that area was divided up from the Ottoman Empire, the Jews got one third of the land for a country called Israel and the Arabs received two thirds in the area called Trans Jordan. That should be enough considering the Palestinians never had a country to begin with. You have to remember that Palestine was not a country but rather just an area of real estate. There were Palestinian Arabs, Palestinian, Jews, and Palestinian Christians. Should there be a country set up for each ethnic group?

It has been claimed that only about 10% of today's Jews can trace their DNA back to Abraham. In 740 AD the people of **Khazaria** (today predominately the country of Georgia between the Black Sea and the Caspian Sea) **converted** to Judaism to protect themselves from attack from the Muslims and Christians. Today they are referred to as **Ashkenazi** Jews when in fact they are not Jews but rather an Asiatic race who converted to the Jewish faith while continuing to speak the **Khazarian** language of **Yiddish** which is completely different from the Hebrew language. These **Khazarian** Jews have no more direct link to the Biblical Abraham than Sammy Davis Junior. All the Prime Ministers of Israel have been Khazarian Jews.

Militant Arab groups want to wipe Israel off the face of the earth. Whereas, the common Arab citizen is more amenable to signing a peace agreement than either the Zionist Israeli Government or militant Arabs. Many Jews want to expand their territory as prophesized in the Bible. Until the Arab militants change their attitude or lose their funding and the Zionist Jews become content with their existing boundaries, it will be impossible to come to any form of peace agreement. Doesn't it seem strange that the U.S. government supports both the Zionists and the Palestinians financially?

Judaism—Jewish Beliefs

I have just read on the Internet some horrible beliefs that are alleged to be in the Talmud and tried without much success to verify this information. Maybe what I found on the Internet was untrue, taken out of context or was mistranslated into English. There is so much information on the internet that it is sometimes difficult to verify. One of my internet sources says "Talmud law permits sexual intercourse between children and adults. (Babylonian Talmud, Tractate Kethuboth 11a Soncino 1961 Edition page 57)" Also it states that you can have sex with an infant 3 years or younger since the hymen will grow back and they will still be considered a virgin. (Hopefully t*his is a test for virginity rather than condoning sex with a child)* Also a mother can have sexual intercourse with her male child as long as he is 9 years old or younger. Hopefully t*his is to emphasize that it is not the fault of the child but would still be considered "child Abuse" by the mother*. It also says that it is ok for a Jew to cheat a Gentile. Just like the other holy books, the Talmud is full of confusing and mixed message passages which are very ungodly.

With this type of information ready available, is it any wonder that anyone who studies the great religions of the world would conclude that their holy books are not divinely inspired?

Talmud

Other references in the Talmudic teachings are:

Erubin 21b. Whoever disobeys the rabbis deserves death and will be punished by being boiled in hot excrement. *(It is claimed by scholars that this is a mistranslation.)*

Moed Kattan 17a. If a person is tempted to do evil he should go to a city where he is not known, dress in black clothes, cover his head in black, and do what his heart desires so that God's name will not be desecrated. *(It could be argued that "Person" doesn't necessarily refer to a Jew, but if so, for whom was the Talmud written?)*

Baba Mezia 114a-114b. Only Jews are human ("only ye are designated men"). Also see Kerithoth 6b under the sub-head, "Oil of Anointing" and berakoth 58a in which **Gentile** women are designated animals (she asses")

Sanhedrin 58b. If a heathen **(Gentile)** hits a Jew, the **Gentile** must be killed. Hitting a Jew is the same as hitting God.

Sanhedrin 57a A Jew need not pay a Gentile ("Cuthean") the wages owed him for work.

Baba Mezia 24a. If a Jew finds an object lost by a **Gentile** ("heathen") it does not need to be returned. (affirmed also in Baba Kamma 113b)

Sanhedrin 57a. When a Jew murders a **Gentile** ("Cuthean") there will be no death penalty. What a Jew steals from a **Gentile** he may keep.

Baba Kamma 113a. Jews may use lies ("subterfuges") to circumvent a **Gentle**. i.e.; Jews may lie to **Gentles.**
Yebhamot 98a. All **Gentile** children are animals.

Abodah Zarah 22a-22b. **Gentiles** prefer sex with cows.

Gittin 69a. To heal his flesh a Jew should take dust that lies within the shadow of an outdoor toilet, mix it with honey and eat it.

Menahoth 43b-44a. A Jewish man is obligated to say the following prayer every day. "Thank you God for not making me a **Gentile**, woman or slave."

Gittin 57b. The Talmud claims that 4 billion Jews were killed by the Romans in the city of Bethar. 58a claims that 16 million Jewish children were wrapped in scrolls and burned alive by the Romans. (Ancient demography indicates that there were not 16 million Jews in the entire world at that time, much less 16 million Jewish children or 4 billion Jews)

*If these quotes from the "Teachings from the Talmud" are true and translated properly, it is no wonder that the Jews have been persecuted. However it would take a **Jewish scholar** to verify all the Anti-Semitic remarks made by people "quoting" the Talmud. It is natural to conclude that with so much hate, apparently in it's teachings about non-Jews that Judaism should not even be considered a legitimate religion. It could be argued that those not used to these Talmudic discussions might be repulsed by the use of euphemisms. It is claimed that the discussion here relates to the dowry for virgins and non-virgins where the female, not being fully active in the sex act with a male minor is not considered to have lost her virginity. The Talmud says that a sexual act between a male adult and a female under the age of three is also **not** considered a loss of virginity (although it is child abuse). Since the girl is too young for her hymen to be broken, she is still considered a virgin. This interpretation is much more believable than believing that the Talmud condones sex with children! But the Talmud does seem to be very un-godly.*

Definition of Religion

Have you ever wondered what the accepted definition of religion was? There is the dictionary definition, and then there is the Internal Revenue Service definition, the philosophers definition and then of course my definition.

One reason we have so many problems today centers around the accepted definitions of religion. None that I could find listed any specific ethics or codes of conduct. You would think this would be the most important aspect of any religious definition. The computer Encarta definition is: "People's beliefs and opinions concerning the existence, nature, and worship of a deity or deities, and divine involvement in the universe and human life." There is no mention of "Ethics" or examples of "Ethics."

The Internal Revenue Service definition could not be found specifically, only court cases involving tax issues for religious organizations and non-profit corporations. A Legal web site gave a definition of "Religious" but not of "Religion." They did state under "religious" that there was a code of ethics"…but didn't actually give any examples. Why is everyone so afraid to describe the meaning of "Ethics" or give examples?

I find it extremely disturbing that none of the definitions include a code of ethics. Shouldn't there be a standard definition of religion by which all religions would have to meet to even be classified as a legitimate religion? My definition of religion would most certainly include a positive relationship with our fellow man no matter what his religious preferences. One would think that everyone's definition of religion would include a code of ethics such as the Ten Commandments as given to the Christians and Jews by the prophet Moses. It certainly would not include the savage treatment of non-Jews and non-Muslims as described in the Talmud and Koran or the killing, raping and plundering as found numerous times in the Christian Bible.

If all religions abided by a high standard of ethics, we would not have the horrible conditions today in the Middle East and around the world. Our current religious beliefs are making life miserable for millions of people.

Maybe it is time to form a new world wide religion based on love and respect of our fellow man by revising the antiquated mythical and superstitious Christian, Jewish and Muslim faiths.

It appears to me that man has made God in man's image rather than the other way around.

Note: More Roger Maynard cartoons at: www.fiddlestix.biz

*Author's note: The elite controllers' use **global warming, energy and food shortages, terrorism, religious conflicts, etc** to control the ignorant masses of the sheeple. Not being able to defend **"Global Warming"**, the elite controllers are now calling it **"Climate Change."***

*"The common enemy of humanity is man. In searching for a <u>new enemy to unite us</u>, we came up with the idea that pollution, the threat of **global warming**, water shortages, famine and the like would fit the bill. All these dangers are caused by human intervention, and it is only through changed attitudes and behavior that they can be overcome. The real enemy then, is humanity itself."*
Richard Haass- Club of Rome- President of the Council on Foreign Relations (CFR)

Quotes by Milton Friedman:

Every friend of freedom must be as revolted as I am by the prospect of turning the United States into an armed camp, by the vision of jails filled with casual drug users and of an army of enforcers empowered to invade the liberty of citizens on slight evidence.

I'm in favor of legalizing drugs. According to my values system, if people want to kill themselves, they have every right to do so. Most of the harm that comes from drugs is because they are illegal.

Governments never learn. Only people learn.

Inflation is taxation without legislation.

Nothing is so permanent as a temporary government program.

The government solution to a problem is usually as bad as the problem.

The Great Depression, like most other periods of severe unemployment, was produced by government mismanagement rather than by any inherent instability of the private economy.

The most important single central fact about a free market is that no exchange takes place unless both parties benefit.

There's no such thing as a free lunch.

Chapter Six
Political Beliefs
Democracy vs. Republic

Most people today don't realize that our country was founded in 1776 as a "Republic" and not as a "Democracy". The word "Democracy" is not even mentioned in the "Declaration of Independence" or the "Constitution". Shortly after signing the "Constitution", a woman was reported as asking Benjamin Franklin what kind of Government were we to have. Franklin said, "A Republic if you can keep it." He was fully aware that it would be constantly attacked by unscrupulous politicians. Even though our pledge of allegiance still says "I pledge allegiance to the flag of the United States of America and to the **Republic** for which it stands..." we have slowly deviated to a **Democracy**.

It is a little difficult to understand the difference between the two types of governments because they both can have some similarities. They can both have an Executive branch, a Legislature and a Judicial branch. The differences used to be taught in school and were even explained in military manuals until about 1928. President Franklin Delano Roosevelt had the description of a "Republic" in the army training manuals taken out and all the remaining manuals were withdrawn from the United States printing office.

Democracy has been described as "Mob rule" (Mobocracy). In other words 51% decide the law and 49% are not represented at all. (Except in a Trial by Jury) Someone once humorously described Democracy as "Three wolves and a sheep deciding what's for dinner." In a Republic 100% of the people are represented by our Constitutional rule of law.

Following is a simple example to explain the difference between a Democracy and a Republic. In a Democracy, a posse of 12 men captures a suspected horse thief and with a vote of 7 to 5 (majority) agrees to hang the man for his crime. (Mob Rule) In other words the opinion of the other 5 in the minority doesn't count. Keep in mind the captured man may not be guilty. Along comes the sheriff before the man is hanged and says, "You can't do that. I am taking this accused man back to town to be tried in a court of law" (Republic). I think most of us would prefer a "Republic" form of Government especially if we found ourselves in the position of being accused of a crime we didn't commit. Also in a Democracy the majority continually elect politicians that advocate spreading the wealth of the working class to the non-working class. Eventually this will destroy the Democratic form of government. This is exactly what is happening to the United States today.

Following are two quotes explaining the evils of democracy:

"Every step.....towards.....democracy is an advance towards destruction...Liberty has never yet lasted long in a democracy; nor has it ever ended in anything better than despotism." (1801) Fisher Ames (1758-1808; Congressman from Massachusetts)

"A Democracy is nothing more than mob rule, where 51% of the people may take away the rights of the other 49%." **Thomas Jefferson**

The following comments are from an unknown author:

Our Republic was never created to be a leveler of men. It was created to be a lifter, a developer of men.

Our Republic was created to let the gifted, the energetic, and the creative rise to new heights of achievement, and to let each man find his own level on the stairway of existence.

Our Republic was created to encourage men to meet their personal responsibilities and to shirk no public duties. That is why our people have always been concerned about the honest needs of their fellow citizens, the chief of these needs being liberty, justice, and opportunity.

Our Republic demands that the nation be governed by the capable, the honorable, the far-seeing, the clear seeing, and not by mediocre men. In the beginning it was so. May it be so again!

Our Republic demands more from men than any other system of self-discipline, dependability, cooperativeness, industry, thrift, and honor. For anyone to foster class consciousness, class conflict, misrepresentation, covetousness, violence, theft, and an open defiance of established law-even when done 'legally'-is to breed anarchy and tyranny.

Our Republic was not designed to interfere with the unalienable right of its people to be masters of their own destinies. Our Republic was established to make men free!"

Party Loyalty

Over the years I have switched back and forth, voting first for a Democrat and then a Republican, basically voting for the man instead of the party. But I know people who would vote for Mickey Mouse if he ran on the party ticket they supported; party loyalty is everything to them. I don't feel that voting for Mickey Mouse is in anyone's best interest. This blind party loyalty insures us that the American people will not be properly represented in our government. It is much easier to participate in **"Blind Political Party Loyalty"** than it is to spend the time and effort to research the various political issues facing us today. Actually, it is just an excuse to **not** get involved.

In the 2008 election, it was obvious that there were millions of people who didn't want to vote for any of the front runners; Hillary Clinton, Barak Obama or John McCain. It would have been nice if each state had added "None of the above" to their ballots, so the dissatisfied voters could be tabulated and reported.

If the Republican Party leaders would wake up and see the enormous number of people that actually supported Ron Paul's views and then made changes in the Republican Party's platform reflecting those views, we would be well on our way to recovery.

Hopefully over the next few years this will happen as more politicians adopt the "Ron Paul Revolution" ideas. If this does not happen soon, I fear the worst is going to happen. The British Statesman and philosopher, Edmund Burke (1729-1797) was quoted as saying, "The only thing necessary for evil to triumph is for good men to do nothing."

As usual, the "hidden controllers" covertly controlled most of the candidates in the 2008 presidential race. When they own all the horses in the race, our "choice" is only an illusion. Ron Paul was an exception. He was a real choice but the majority of the American voters tragically failed to support him. A very large percentage of the people I have talked to who at my suggestion, took the time and trouble to research his message said, "I had no idea any politician believed like that. He sounds fantastic. Certainly I will support him." The problem was not enough people were knowledgeable as to what his political platform was. The controlled mass media and the so called "pundits" made sure Ron Paul's message was minimized.

I have always felt closer to the Republican conservative philosophy but the last few years felt like the old Republican Party had died. It not only died with the election of George Bush and Dick Cheney but was converted into almost a dictatorial type of government with Bush bypassing our Congress to go to war with Iraq, enacting the Patriot Act and using Executive orders instead of abiding by the U.S. Constitution. It reminds me of the steps that Hitler took prior to becoming Germany's leader. It got even worse when Nancy Pelosi and Harry Reid failed to uphold their campaign promises, both to end the war in Iraq immediately and to proceed with impeachment proceedings against Bush and Cheney. Their failures to reestablish the powers of Congress will continue to haunt us well into the future. I only hope that their failure to honor their campaign promises was not influenced by any personal threats they may have received to themselves or family members. The American people are so dissatisfied with Congress today that they have only a 10% approval rating. It is becoming more and more obvious to me that the "global elite" control both the Republicans **and** the Democrats.

Republican Congressman Ron Paul

In 2007 when I first heard about Ron Paul, I for the first time in years felt that we finally had found an honest politician who would return this country to one that would abide by the Constitution. I felt like Ron Paul was of the same caliber as George Washington, Thomas Jefferson and Benjamin Franklin. It is disappointing to me that the brainwashed people of this country failed to see that Dr Paul's platform was exactly what was needed to get us out of the mess we are in. Unfortunately, the banksters and the controlled mass media would win again!

Dr. Paul represents the 70% of the people who want us to withdraw from Iraq and Afghanistan immediately. He promised that we would no longer be the policeman of the world and would immediately bring our troops home from the other military bases we have around the world. This would save us hundreds of billions of dollars that we could use to protect our own borders and assist the poor citizens of this country. He explained how he would get rid of the **"Individual Income Tax"** which only goes to pay the private bankers- and replace it with **nothing**. He knows that for this country to remain strong and to protect the rights of the people, the President and Congress must abide by our Constitution.

The people of this great nation missed the opportunity to elect a President that would save our nation from the evils of the Federal Reserve System and stop the insane idea that the U.S. must police the world. The controlled mass media and the banking interests made sure that the public knew very little about this giant of a man. By marginalizing his message and giving him little TV and newspaper coverage, Ron Paul was not elected our president in 2008. I feel disgusted and sad to think that we are not really represented in the U.S. political system. He is continuing the "Ron Paul Revolution" through the "Campaign for Liberty" group where the millions of his supporters will carry on his work. Hopefully the necessary changes will be made gradually and peaceably as more and more politicians adopt the "Ron Paul Revolution" ideology.

Electoral College

The President and Vice President of the United States are elected by what is called the "Electoral College", rather than by the popular vote. Instead of voting directly for the President and Vice president, the U.S. citizen casts votes for representatives called "electors." The electors are free to vote for the candidate of their choice- however, they normally are pledged to vote for specific candidates; the same as the constituents in their area. Therefore, the public indirectly votes for the President and Vice president by voting for the pledged electors. The Electoral College is composed of 538 electors; each state has a number of electors equal to the number of its Senators and Representatives plus three for the District of Columbia.

At the beginning of our young nation, when many of our citizens could neither read nor write, the Electoral College may have served the purpose of ensuring that a qualified candidate would be elected for such a high office. However, with today's communication system and education of the electorate, it is no longer necessary to use this antiquated and unfair system. Why not replace our out-dated electoral college with the popular vote and allow as many as 10 to 15 candidates to run for president? What would be wrong for each party to have three or four candidates running for president in the November election and allowing the American public to vote directly for their choice; each with their own separate platform? Think how difficult it would be for the "lobbyists" and "banksters" to control that many different candidates- plus the electorate would be better represented by having a choice of platforms.

Vote fraud

It is extremely important to elect a president and congressional leaders that will reverse all of the unconstitutional programs enacted by George Bush and Dick Cheney; particularly the "Patriot Act." We have gone from the Department of War (1789-1947), to The Department of Defense (1949) to George Bush's Department of **Offense.** The United States has strayed far from the vision of our wise founding fathers. Meaningful changes will not happen unless we get an honest voting system established. In each election there is suspicion of vote fraud and it doesn't appear that anyone, republican or democrat, wants to take on the challenge to fix it. There were accusations of voting machine fraud in the Iowa Caucus and the New Hampshire primaries in 2008 when votes for Ron Paul were not tabulated correctly. There is still a large portion of Americans who believe that Al Gore was not allowed to be elected our president because of the fraud connected to the 'Hanging Chad' fiasco. It has been proven that the electronic voting machines made by companies like "Diebold" are easily rigged but no one seems to know how to make them tamper proof.

One possible solution would be to have each ballot printed with a reference number. There would be three ballot copies: one stays with the precinct, one goes to the state headquarters for the official count and one to the voter. The next day, the voter if he or she wishes, could verify the accuracy of their vote by viewing their voting record by reference number on a computer web site. This procedure should be able to be done in such a manner so as to make it extremely difficult to alter the election count.

Texas Vote Count Doesn't Add Up

Written by a Ron Paul supporter:

"They want us to believe that McCain won Texas in a landslide. A place where I have never heard anyone mention his name, never seen so much as a bumper sticker, and clearly a state that is covered by Ron Paul signs. Just for the sake of discussion, let's say it's possible."

What I find seriously hard to believe is this:

Ron Paul got 70% of the vote in his district for Congress. 37,220 votes. But… In that same district they want us to believe he only got 6,697 Votes for President."

Could it be possible that there is a concerted effort to **not** fix the fraud problem? This could be the final solution that the elite controllers use to alter the voting records when their preferred candidate looks as if they are not going to win.

Joseph Stalin was reported as saying, "Those that vote decide nothing. Those that count the votes decide everything."

Inflation

Just as important as protecting our country from foreign invaders, it is equally important for our government to adopt sound monetary policies that protect the value of our dollar. The way to do this is to abolish the Federal Reserve and the fractional reserve banking practice. Then allow our government to print its own money as provided for in the Constitution, **without** incurring any interest to a private bank.

Because the unconstitutional Federal Reserve, which was adopted in 1913, charges us unnecessary interest, the value of the dollar has dropped by 97 percent. This is an actual theft by the private Federal Reserve bankers perpetrated against the American people.

Following is a simplified explanation that will attempt to explain the concept of inflation. When I was growing up in the 1950's and gas was $.25 a gallon a **silver dollar** would buy four gallons of gas. Today in 2008 a silver dollar is worth about $18.00 and will still buy four gallons of gas with a little left over. A **paper dollar** will not even buy one gallon of gas. So, ask yourself, "Has the price of gas gone up or has the purchasing value of the paper dollar gone down?" There are several factors that have caused gas prices to increase, but Wall Street price speculators and inflation are the main cause.

Doesn't it seem logical that our government has the responsibility to protect the value of our paper money? Shouldn't I be able to put a dollar bill under my mattress today and pull it out 20 years later and buy the same amount of goods and services? Instead, our government allows the private Federal Reserve Bank to create more and more fiat money further eroding the value of the existing dollars. This has to stop!

Let me explain how the creating of more money without any backing from "additional labor" or "value added" affects the value of the existing money. It is really quite simple. If the Federal Reserve System doubled the supply of money, the existing value of our money, whatever that is, would now be worth half as much. What do you think the effect will be on our money value today when our government creates more money for the government economic stimulus checks and the bank bailouts? The purpose of this money is to stimulate the economy and keep the banks from collapsing, but in reality this is only a temporary Band-Aid and will only increase the inflation of our paper dollars which will result in even higher prices.

When people complain to me that the price of everything is going up, I reply, "The purchasing value of the dollar is going down" causing the price of goods and services to go up.

The politicians would rather finance their wars and pork projects through inflation rather than raising taxes. When they raise taxes the public understands this and immediately feels the pain and votes them out of office. But when they allow more money to be created to finance government expenses, the public doesn't understand what has been done to them. They know prices keep going up but do not understand why. In reality the purchasing value of the dollar has gone down. They don't understand that "Inflation" is nothing more than a tax; a hidden tax that lowers the quality of life for each of us. (Except for the elite bankers and super rich)

Fractional Reserve Banking

Banks are allowed to loan out more money than they have on deposit. The results of this are that the banks have created 9-10 times more money than they have assets to cover. This further inflates the money supply and causes more inflation. The banks profit and the consumers pay higher and higher prices for consumer goods because of inflation. This practice would be considered counterfeiting if anyone else tried it.

The Federal Reserve

The Federal Reserve System is one of the biggest frauds ever perpetrated against the American people. It is **not Federal** and they have **no reserves!** It was enacted in 1913 to once again establish a private central bank of the United States of America and was signed into law by President Woodrow Wilson. The 16th amendment to our Constitution, also enacted in 1913, authorized unapportioned Federal Taxes on income. **What a coincidence these were passed at the same time!** Apparently few people were concerned because at this time not very many paid income tax. But the door was now open to allow the Federal Government to gradually raise the income tax to include almost every American citizen. This was the start of expanding the size of our Federal Government way beyond what our founding fathers intended and greatly diminishing the rights of us citizens.

Our Constitution states that **Congress** is to be the one to coin our money and regulate its value. However, the bankers met secretly in 1910 on Jekyll Island, Georgia to draw up the Federal Reserve Act. They unconstitutionally gave themselves the power to print our money and loan it back to us with interest, without oversight from our Congress. It is not in the best interest of the people to have money creation delegated to a private bank. It should be clear to everyone that the private Federal Reserve System is unconstitutional. Even economists like Milton Freedman have written about the evils of the Federal Reserve System.

It is really not that hard to abolish the Federal Reserve especially if you do not value your life or political career. It would be extremely difficult to enact legislation to abolish it. However, according to the original agreement, the stock issued could be bought back, effectively putting it out of business. But an easier way would be to do what John F Kennedy did. We could start issuing **interest free** Treasury notes instead of **interest bearing**

Federal Reserve Notes and gradually replace the FRS notes until in a few years there would be none left.

Private vs. Government Control of America's Money

Following are some comments made by past presidents, congressmen and others regarding the control of our money supply:

"If the American People ever allow private banks to control the issue of their currency, first by inflation, then by deflation, the banks ...will deprive the people of all property until their children wake up homeless on the continent their fathers conquered...The issuing power should be taken from the banks and restored to the people, to whom it properly belongs."—*Thomas Jefferson*

"I sincerely believe that banking institutions are more dangerous to our liberties than standing armies. Already they have raised up a money aristocracy that has set the government at defiance." -- *Thomas Jefferson*

"History records that the money changers have used every form of abuse, intrigue, deceit, and violent means possible to maintain their control over governments by controlling money and its issuance."—*James Madison*

"If Congress has the right under the Constitution to issue paper money, it was given them to use themselves, not to be delegated to individuals or corporations."—*Andrew Jackson*

"The Government should create, issue, and circulate all the currency and credits needed to satisfy the spending power of the Government and the buying power of consumers. By the adoption of these principles, the taxpayers will be saved immense sums of interest. Money will cease to be master and become the servant of humanity."—*Abraham Lincoln*

"It is well enough that the people of the nation do not understand our banking and monetary system, for if they did, I believe there would be a revolution before tomorrow morning."—**Henry Ford**

"Let me issue and control a nation's money and I care not who writes the laws."—**Mayer Rothschild**

"The financial system ...has been turned over to the Federal Reserve board, that board administers the finance system by authority of...a purely profiteering group. The system is private, conducted for the sole purpose of obtaining the greatest possible profits from the use of other people's money." *(1923) Charles A. Lindberg, a Republican Representative from Minnesota, the father of famed aviator "Lucky Lindy."*

"We have in this country one of the most corrupt institutions the world has ever known. I refer to the Federal Reserve Board...This evil institution has impoverished...the people of the United States...and has practically bankrupted our government. It has done this through...the corrupt practices of the moneyed vultures who control it." *(1932) Louis T. McFadden (Republican Congressman from Pennsylvania*

"Most Americans have no real understanding of the operations of the international moneylenders...The accounts of the Federal Reserve System have never been audited. It operates outside the control of Congress and... manipulates the credit of the United States." *Senator Barry Goldwater*

Term Limits for Our Legislature

Polls that have been taken over the last several years show that 65-80% of the voters would like to see a constitutional amendment passed to establish term limits for our congressmen. Some states have even passed their own laws establishing term limits but a Supreme Court ruling has said that states cannot impose term limits for Congress. This Supreme Court decision ensures that the lobbyist and elite bankers will be able to continue controlling our long term professional representatives.

So why don't we have term limits? Shouldn't everyone agree that a **citizen** politician in office for a short time would better represent the voters than that of a **professional** politician that is in office for life? It is understandable that no one currently in Congress would vote to limit their own terms.

It would be much easier to pass such a bill if it **excluded** current incumbents of both houses as long as they are reelected successively. The newly elected representatives would only be allowed to serve for a total of 12 years- the Senate, 2 six year terms and the House, 6 two year terms.

Up till about 40 years ago, Congressional turnover was about 50%. However during the last 15 years it has come down to about 10%. *(Reference Nelson Walker's web site, Useless-Knowledge.com)*

The House of Representatives have members that have been there for over 50 years. Is this really in the best interest of the American people?

There would be many advantages to "term limits", including the following: (1) It would reduce the lobbyists' influence (2) It would replace **career** politicians with **citizen** politicians (3) The quality of legislation would be improved (4) Hopefully it would result in a smaller, more efficient government.

All of us should be actively contacting our representatives encouraging them to vote on an amendment to the Constitution establishing term limits. This isn't a new idea. Both the Greeks and Romans imposed term limits on certain offices and George Washington and Thomas Jefferson argued in support of term limits.

When democracy granted democratic methods to us in times of opposition, this was bound to happen in a democratic system. However, we National Socialists never asserted that we represented a democratic point of view, but we have declared openly that we used the democratic methods only to gain power and that, <u>after assuming the power, we would deny to our adversaries without any consideration the means which were granted to us in times of our opposition.</u>
 Joseph Paul Goebbels *(1897-1945) German Nazi Minister of Propaganda*

*What is the difference between the **National Debt** and the **Annual Federal Budget Deficit?** Politicians continually talk about having a **balanced budget** (expenses equal to revenue) but almost never talk about paying off the **National Debt** because under our present monetary system, the private Federal Reserve Banking system makes it virtually impossible to ever pay off the debt.*

***National Debt**-This is the difference between the amount of money that our country has ever spent since 1776 less what it has collected in taxes, tariffs, etc. since 1776.*

***Annual Federal Budget**-This is calculated each year. It is the difference between what the Federal Government spends and the revenue it receives. If it is a surplus it reduces the national debt but if it is a deficit, it adds to the amount of the national debt.*

PRESIDENT-ELECT BARACK OBAMA'S TAX PLAN:

LOOK, HE'S GIVING US ALL MONEY, JUST LIKE HE PROMISED!

HE HAS YOUR WALLET.

Note: More Roger Maynard cartoons at: www.fiddlestix.biz

Chapter Seven
History of Money and Banking

The first bankers were the **goldsmiths** who accepted bullion and coins for safe keeping and would give the owner a receipt for his deposit. The owner soon discovered that it was easier to use his receipt to pay for goods and services than to use the actual gold. Since the receipt holders rarely demanded their gold all at the same time, the goldsmiths realized they could profit enormously by making more loans than they had gold on hand. Gradually the goldsmiths became bankers as they stopped manufacturing gold items and replaced it with lending activities. In this way banks began to create money. This was the beginning of our modern banking system.

The book *I Bet You Thought*, published by the Federal Reserve Bank of New York says:

"Money is any generally accepted medium of exchange, not simply coin and currency. **Money doesn't have to be intrinsically valuable, be issued by a government or be in any special form."**

Privately issued forms of money only require public confidence to be accepted as money. Counterfeit money is also money as long as nobody discovers it is counterfeit. Likewise, "bad" checks pass as money as long as no one objects. Once the truth is discovered, the value of such "phony money", like bad checks, ceases to exist.

When a person deposits money in a bank, this money is that person's asset and the bank's liability. There is no law that gives banks the authority to create money by lending their liabilities. (Fractional Reserve Banking). If you or I did this, it would be called "counterfeiting" and we would be put in jail.

Consider money as a receipt for your labor or as a receipt for you adding additional value to a product or service. For example, after working 8 hours, your boss gives you a receipt for 8 hours of labor. This receipt is proof that you have added something to the monetary system. You should be able to trade this receipt (money) for other goods and services and the recipient should be able to again trade this same receipt for goods and services. If someone counterfeits a receipt or as in the case of the Federal Reserve-simply prints more receipts without any work being done or value added, the existing receipts have been devalued and are worth less. We call this devaluation "Inflation."

An excellent 3 ½ hour documentary on this subject is "The Money Masters" produced by, the "Royalty Production Company" P. O. Box 909, Immokalee, Florida 34143. It was made in 1998 but the information is still relevant today. It is about the worldwide history of central banking and fractional reserve lending. You can either buy the DVD or download it off the internet. I highly recommend everyone view it.

Historic Time Line of the International Banking Empire

1744--Mayer Amschel Bauer, born in Frankfurt Germany, was the son of Moses Amschel Bauer, a goldsmith and money lender. Young Mayer Bauer possessed an immense intellectual ability which motivated his father to teach him all he could about the money and lending business. His father had hoped to have his son become a Rabbi, but died before his plans could be fulfilled.

A few years later Mayer Amschel Bauer became a junior partner in a bank owned by the Oppenheimers in Hanover. He later returned to Frankfurt and purchased the business his father had started in 1750. He decided to change his name to "Rothschild." His father had adopted the red shield emblem from the red flag which was the emblem of the revolutionary minded Jews in Eastern Europe. The word "Rothschild" literally means red shield.

1769--Early in his banking career, Mayer Amschel Rothschild learned how to gain acceptance with the local leaders. In September 1769 he was able to hang a sign above his shop bearing the arms of Hess-Hanau. In gold letters it read, "M.A. Rothschild by Appointment Court Factor to His Imperial Highness, Prince William of Hanau."

1770-- Mayer Rothschild married Gutele Schnaper, age seventeen. They had five daughters and five sons. The sons were Amschel, Salomon, Nathan, Kalmann, and Jacob.

It has been reported that Rothschild embezzled $3,000,000 from Prince William who had embezzled it from his own troops. With this huge influx of capital, Rothschild was able to become the first international banker. (Reference the *Jewish Encyclopedia*, 1905 Edition.)

Mayer gave his son Nathan the $3,000,000 and sent him to London as a merchant banker. With the huge profit Nathan realized from investing in gold from the East India Company, the Rothschild's were on their way to becoming the most wealthy international banking company in the world.

The Rothschild's began building their banking empire by establishing branches in five European cities—London, Berlin, Vienna, Paris, and Naples--where a son was placed in charge of each branch. The main headquarters of "The House of Rothschild" is to this day located in London England with branches in the United States and most countries throughout the world.   It is difficult to prove the extent of their influence and control due to subsidiaries with different names and lack of exposure in the banking world. It appears that there are only five countries whose central bank is **not** controlled by the Rothschilds- Iran, North Korea, Sudan, Cuba, and Libya. Is it a coincidence that these countries are the same countries that are enemies of the United States and Britain?

1791--First Bank of the United States (First private bank in charge of our nation's money supply)

1811—Congress voted to abandon the "First Bank of the United States and its charter.

1812--Mayer Amschel Rothschild died September 19, 1812. Biographer Frederic Morton, in his book "The Rothschild's" says that Mayer Amschel Rothschild and his five sons were "wizards" of finance and "fiendish calculators" who were motivated by a "demonic drive" to succeed in their secret undertakings.

1815--Some historians say that Nathan Rothschild made a huge fortune by using privileged information regarding the outcome of the "Battle of Waterloo." However, in Niall Ferguson's book, "Money's Prophets', he states that this is a myth. "The Rothschild's courier did alert them first to Napoleons' defeat, but since they had bet big on a protracted military campaign, any quick gains in bonds after waterloo were too small to offset the disruption to their business." The reader will have to make up their own minds as to which version of the story is true.

1816—Second Bank of the United States chartered (<u>Second private bank in charge of our nation's money supply)</u>

1820--After 1820, Nathan Rothschild had control of the Bank of England. He is reported to have said, "The man who controls Britain's money supply controls the British Empire, and I control the British money supply."

1820--From the 1820's through the 1830's the Rothschild's became involved in the financial affairs of the United States. Through their agent, Nicholas Biddle, they attempted to defeat Andrew Jackson's move to abolish the international bankers. Jackson struck back by vetoing the move to renew the charter of the "Bank of the United States" which was a central bank controlled by the international bankers. Jackson won- in 1836 the bank went out of business. The Rothschild's had lost the first round. I don't believe that it was a coincidence that there was an assassination attempt on Andrew Jackson's life after the Bank Charter was not renewed.

1836—Second Bank of the United States chartered expired. President Andrew Jackson had successfully killed the bank. (Jackson's tombstone proudly states- "I killed the bank.")

1860--South Carolina succeeded from the Union on December 29. Within a few weeks another six states joined the succession from the Union to form the Confederate States of America with Jefferson Davis as President.

1861--In December 1861, British, French, and Spanish troops landed in Mexico in defiance of the Monroe Doctrine to aid the Confederacy. Abraham Lincoln appealed for help from Russia, Britain's enemy, for assistance. A Russian fleet under Admiral Liviski landed in New York harbor on September 24, 1863 and Admiral Popov landed his fleet in San Francisco on October 12. This caused England and France to hesitate in getting involved in America's Civil War just long enough to favor the North. Once again, the Rothschild's applied their cunning instincts to make money by financing both sides of a conflict. It has been reported that they would loan slightly more money to the side they wanted to win and then require both sides to guarantee the debts of the losing party. I suppose they made even more money in financing loans for reconstruction after the war. I have often wondered how history would have been changed if countries could not have gotten financing for their unnecessary wars.

Rather than pay the Rothschilds the exorbitant amount of interest they demanded, Lincoln issued constitutional, interest free, United States notes (Greenbacks) to finance the Civil War. Some historians believe this is why Lincoln was assassinated on April 14, 1865 by John Wilkes Booth. Had the international bankers been involved with Lincoln's assassination? Izola Forrester, Booths granddaughter, stated that her grandfather had been in close contact with a mysterious European prior to the assassination and had made at least one trip to Europe. Many people at the time believed that Booth was not the person that died in the fire and that he lived for several years after the assassination. An attempt to verify the body of Booth by modern DNA tests was rejected a few years ago.

1862—The congress of the United States enacted the first income tax law to help finance the Civil War.

Not being successful in dividing the United States by intervening in our Civil War, the Rothschild's financed John D. Rockefeller to help expand Standard Oil. They also financed Andrew Carnegie's steel business and Edward Harriman's railroad company. One way or another they were going to exert a great deal of influence in America's financial affairs.

1868—Congress focused its taxation efforts on tobacco and alcohol and eliminated the income tax in 1872. It had a short lived revival in 1894 and 1895. The U.S. Supreme Court ruled that the income tax was unconstitutional since it was not apportioned among the states as required by the Constitution.

1871--Albert Pike, in a letter to Giuseppe Mazzini, stated that a planned First World War was to be implemented in order to destroy Czarist Russia, and to place them under the control of the "Illuminati." Russia was then to be used as the "**Bogey Man**." It sounds a lot like what President Bush and the CIA has done in creating "al Qaeda", and declaring Osama Bin Laden the terrorist **"Bogey Man."** *(It looks like history does keep repeating itself.)*

1907--Jacob Schiff, the boss of the Rothschild owned Kuhn, Loeb and Company, made a speech to the New York Chamber of Commerce warning them that unless the United States had a private central bank with adequate controls of credit resources, the country would experience the most severe money panic in its history. Sure enough, the United States experienced a money crisis that some historians believed was caused by the Rothschilds. The crisis made billions of dollars for the bankers while destroying the life savings of millions of ordinary American citizens. The stage had been set. Now the American people could be deceived into supporting a private central bank (The Federal Reserve System) and the 16th Amendment authorizing income tax on individual's salaries.

1913—The 16th Amendment was passed on February 3rd and the Federal Reserve Act was passed on December 23. Once again, we had an invisible unaccountable private bank. The bankers had more power and control over the American citizen than our elected government representatives. **This unconstitutional banking act**

<u>and income tax amendment is one of the biggest crimes ever committed against the American people.</u>

For the international bankers to achieve their goal of world domination, they use deceptive tactics to eliminate the old world and establish a **New World Order**.

The First World War, with all its casualties, was intended to demoralize the American citizens to the point of them demanding a solution to the world wide conflict. The League of Nations was pushed by President Wilson but didn't take hold. So a second world war was planned in order to bring about a world government and policing body organization. They succeeded with the establishment of the United Nations in 1945. This was a major step in establishing the "New World Order" controlled by the international bankers.

1941--World War ll was to be implemented by taking advantage of the differences that existed between Zionist and the German Nationalists. One result of this would be the establishment of the State of Israel in Palestine.

Some people think we are now in the third world war to take advantage of the differences between the Zionists and Arabs; making money for the bankers, military industrial complex companies and oil companies. Also some of the elites must consider that war is an efficient means of population control. (Eugenics)

Gold Standard

When I first began my research for this book three years ago, like many people, I assumed that if our country would just return to the "Gold Standard", everything would be all right. The more I studied our monetary policies operating under the Federal Reserve System with its fractional reserve banking, I became convinced that we definitely need to abolish them but we do **not** need to have our money backed by gold, silver or even petroleum.

Keep in mind that the same unscrupulous bankers also control much of the gold, silver and petroleum. However, almost everyone I talk to disagrees including most economists and the so called TV news personalities. They **incorrectly** believe that our money must be backed by gold or silver. The TV news programs and newspapers never discuss the possibility that the Federal Reserve is the main problem causing the monetary crisis or that our money does not need any backing other than the government accepting it for payment of taxes. It is no wonder that the public's opinion in this area is completely distorted.

Our original 13 colonies issued interest free paper money that was not backed by anything and it was extremely successful until King George the III stopped it. Our young country did not have any large amounts of gold until the 1849 gold rush. Abraham Lincoln successfully issued interest free paper money called "Green Backs" with no precious metal backing, to finance the Civil War. None of these examples seem to sway the opinions of people today because they have been brainwashed by the elite bankers and the controlled news media.

Ellen Hodgson Brown, author of the book, "The Web of Debt" explains very clearly how Adolph Hitler got Germany out of a severe depression when he came to power in 1933. Germany's economy was in total disarray because of ruinous World War I war-reparation obligations and he was unable to get foreign investments or credit from the international bankers. By printing his own debt free paper money, in four years, he was able to develop Germany into the strongest economy in Europe. Hitler was able to finance Germany's entire government and war effort from 1935 to 1945 without gold or debt from the private banks.

The international bankers felt they had to put a stop to Hitler before he influenced other countries by showing them how successful they could be by printing their own debt free money without any gold or silver backing. Ellen Hodgson Brown says in her book, *"....and it took the whole Capitalist and Communist world to destroy the German power over Europe and bring Europe back under the heel of the bankers. Such history of money does not appear in the textbooks of public (government) schools today."*

The evil banking practices of the unnecessary Federal Reserve System is the greatest secret ever to be kept from the American people. If you do not get anything else out of reading this book, please understand that the Federal Reserve System and fractional reserve banking must be abolished and a monetary system ***does not*** need to be backed by gold or silver.

The "behind the scenes" actions of the international bankers are made for their financial profit and control of the entire world. The controlled news media and their celebrity hosts are the same as **"traitors"** for not exposing the bankers for what they really do.

Wall Street

I have often thought that it would be more appropriate for "Wall Street" to be located in Las Vegas. For example it has been reported that at any one time there is as much as 100 times the amount of trading in gold and silver than there is actual **physical** gold and silver. Trading in gold, silver and currencies that you don't own is the same as high risk gambling! Also such financial activity as multiple **speculative** commodity trading, short selling, future contracts, margin calls, options, puts, derivatives, hedge funds, etc are nothing more than legalized gambling.

Many people partially blamed the 1929 crash on the investment banks high risk financial activity and therefore enacted the Glass-Steagall Act of 1933 as an attempt to separate commercial banking from investment banking. An investment bank is a financial institution that (1) raises capital (2) trades in securities and (3) manages corporate mergers and acquisitions. A commercial bank is the one that is most familiar to the public in that it is where we keep our checking accounts, savings, and go for loans to finance our homes and businesses. It was deemed a conflict of interest for commercial banks to be involved in investment banking especially when the bank used their depositor's money for investments.

In 1999 the Glass Steagall was partially repealed and once again restrictions on banking activities were not as severely limited allowing the investment banks to engage in more risky financial transactions. That is when the phrase, "Too big to fail" originated that resulted in the trillion dollar investment bank bailouts. In effect the taxpayer was underwriting the investment banks gambling losses and paying the huge bonuses to the executives of these banks for doing a lousy job and in some cases rewarding them for criminal activity.

More than anything else, multiple **speculative** commodity trades are responsible for the high cost of gasoline and food products. Third world countries' people, who are already below the poverty line, are now starving because of the high price of food.

It is understandable that a small farmer does not directly sell his 10 loads of corn to General Mills. To be cost effective, General Mills needs to buy the corn in thousands of tons to be shipped to their processing plants. The middle man (not a trader), the grain elevator owners, buys from multiple farmers and then ships in bulk to companies like General Mills. The elevator operator has added a valuable service to the process by grouping small purchases and storing them until there is enough volume to be economically shipped to the processing plant. But when a similar type of transaction goes through multiple **traders-** sometimes up to 20-30 times utilizing these exotic trading practices- no value at all is added to the product—only extra cost to the consumer. There are legitimate commodity trades where a trader will buy large quantities of a product and add value to the commodity by making it available to others wanting to buy in smaller quantities. It's the unnecessary multiple trades that don't add any value to a commodity- only costs, that cause prices to the consumer to increase.

The politicians keep blaming the necessity of the 700 billion dollar bank bailout in October, 2008 on the deregulation of Wall Street. (Bloomberg and others have admitted that this "bailout" has increased to 9.7 trillion dollars) Other than basic stock trading, maybe all these other exotic trading practices mentioned above should be regulated to the extent of making them illegal.

Third world countries' entire monetary systems have been destroyed by these unscrupulous investment transactions; and now it is destroying the American economy. In fact, the entire world's economy is plagued by the Las Vegas type speculations on the stock exchanges, the manipulation of currencies, and the continual unnecessary wars that are financed by the elite bankers and Wall Street investors. The Wall Street investors and the corporate predators get richer and the common man gets poorer and poorer.

The Juror has more power than the President of the United States and Congress.
Reference Lysander Spoonser's essay.

It is left, therefore, to the juries; if they think the permanent judges are under any bias whatever in any cause, to take on themselves to <u>judge the law</u> as well as the fact. They never exercise this power but when they suspect partiality in the judges, and by the exercise of this power they have been the firmest bulwarks of English liberty.
Thomas Jefferson

"The jury has a right to <u>judge both the law as well as the fact in controversy."</u>
John Jay, 1st Chief Justice U.S. Supreme Court, 1789

Chapter Eight
Trial by Jury

The Sixth Amendment to the United States Constitution and every state constitution states that in all criminal prosecutions, the accused shall enjoy the right to a speedy and public trial, by an impartial jury wherein the crime shall have been committed.

Not all criminal cases require a jury trial. The Supreme Court has consistently excluded "Petty Offenses." from triggering this right.

The jurors are recruited from the general population and chosen at random. It convenes them for the purpose of one particular trial and entrusts them with great official powers of decision. It permits them to carry on deliberations in secret and to report their final judgment **without giving reasons** for it. After their service to the state is completed they are ordered to disband and return to private life.

Lysander Spooner's essay in 1852 stated that this was the final **Check and Balance** of guarding against a tyrannical government. Spooner wrote, among other things, the Jury should have the power to question the legality of the law and determine if it applied to a particular case. (Jury Nullification)

It has been said that the juror has more power than the President of the United States and Congress. For example, If only one juror votes, **"Not Guilty,"** there is no conviction. The problem we have today is that some judges fail to inform the jurors of their rights.

The **Minneapolis Star and Tribune** on November 30, 1984 printed an article entitled:

"What Judges Don't Tell the Jurors?"

At the time of the adoption of the Constitution, the jury's role as defense against political oppression was unquestioned in America jurisprudence. This nation survived until the 1850's, when prosecutions under the Fugitive Slave Act were largely unsuccessful because juries refused to convict.

Then judges began to erode the institutions of free juries, leading to the absurd compromise that is the current state of the law. While our courts uniformly state juries have the power to return a verdict of not guilty whatever the facts, they routinely tell the jurors the opposite.

Further the courts will not allow the defendants or their council to inform the jurors of their true power. A lawyer who made... Hamilton's argument would face professional discipline and charges of contempt of court.

By what logic should juries have the power to acquit a defendant but no right to know about that power? The courts decisions that have suppressed the notion of jury nullification cannot resolve this paradox.

More than logic has suffered. As was originally conceived, juries were to be a kind of safety valve, a way to soften the bureaucratic rigidity of the judicial system by introducing the common sense of community. If they are to function effectively as the 'conscience of the community,' the jurors must be told that they have the power and the right to say no to a prosecution in order to achieve a greater good. To cut jurors off from this information is to undermine one of the most important institutions.

Perhaps the community should educate itself. Then citizens called for jury duty could teach the judges a needed lesson in civics. **From the Minneapolis Star and Tribune November 30, 1984.**

Some would argue that the jurors cannot always be relied upon to make the correct decision as to whether the defendant is innocent or guilty. I would argue the same problem exists with the judge making the final decision. If there is any possible chance that an error could be made, I would rather take the chance of having 12 jurors of the defendant's peers make the mistake rather than one biased judge. The important point to be made here is that the 12 jurors are the final "Check and Balance" of a possible tyrannical government, a tyrannical unjust law or a tyrannical unjust judge!

A law which violates the Constitution is not valid:

"The jury has a right to judge both the law as well as the fact in controversy." John Jay, 1st Chief Justice U.S. Supreme Court, 1789

"The jury has the right to determine both the law and the facts." Samuel Chase, U.S. Supreme Court Justice, 1796.

"The jury has the power to bring a verdict in the teeth of both law and fact." Oliver Wendell Holmes U.S. Supreme Court Justice, 1902

"The law itself is on trial quite as much as the cause which is to be decided." Harlan F. Stone, 12th Chief Justice U.S. Supreme Court, 1941.

"The pages of history shine on instances of the jury's exercise of its prerogative to disregard instructions of the judge..." U.S. vs. Dougherty, 473 F 2nd 1113, 1139, 1972.

"All laws which are repugnant to the Constitution are null and void." Marburg vs. Madison, 5 US (2 Cranch) 137, 174, 176, 1803

"An unconstitutional Act is not law; it confers no rights; it imposes no duties; affords no protection; it creates no office; it is in legal contemplation, as inoperative as though it had never been passed." Norton vs. Shelby County 118US 425 p. 442

"No one is bound to obey an unconstitutional law and no courts are bound to enforce it." 16 Am Jur 2d, Sec 177 late 2d, Sec 256

"The general rule is that an unconstitutional statute, though having the form and name of law, is in reality no law, but is wholly void and ineffective for any purpose; since it unconstitutionally dates from the time of its enactment and not merely from the date of the decision so banning it." Quote from **"The Citizens Rule Book"** available from **INFOWARS .com.**

Don't allow the politicians, judges, lawyers and bureaucrats to take the power away from you when you serve as a juror.

Warning: You will probably be disqualified as a juror if you reveal your understanding of the juror's rights before being selected as a juror. During the selection process the defense attorney would surely select you but the prosecuting attorney would not. The judge may even find the defense attorney in contempt of court if he reveals his views concerning the constitutional rights of the jurors.

It is everyone's civic duty to volunteer as a juror. However, if for some reason you don't want to be selected you could either explain to the judge your understanding of the jurors' rights as described above or simply advise the court that you can tell whether a person is guilty or innocent just by looking at them. Of course this second scenario is not true but both will work to keep you from being selected as a juror.

Chapter Nine
The Draft vs. a Volunteer Army

Before reading Ron Paul's book, *Freedom Under Siege*, I had never considered that the draft might be unconstitutional. It only makes sense that if our government needs a military force, it must have the right to draft people and finance such a force to protect our country. Some people argue that the draft, "conscription", is authorized by our Constitution. They say that it is authorized by Article 1, Section 8, Clauses 1, 12, 13, and 14. It says "Congress shall have the power ...to provide for the common defense and general welfare for the United States...to raise and support armies." Note: That there is no mention of Congress having the power to **forcibly** conscript an individual.

When the Viet Nam War started in 1959, many of my friends were volunteering for military service because they said they would probably be drafted anyway. I decided not to volunteer because (1) I thought we were wrong to go to war and (2) I could not see myself killing someone who was doing for their country the same as my country was requiring me to do. I felt sure I would die for nothing; not defending my country but for fighting for a cause that I did not understand or think was justifiable. It just didn't make any sense to me particularly because the Vietnamese were not a threat to the United States. When the Gulf of Tonkin incident happened in 1964, I didn't know at the time that it was a complete fabrication by President Lyndon Johnson.

As it turned out, I was never drafted. When my time came to be drafted there was an exemption if you were attending college. I had just enrolled at The University of Kansas majoring in Electrical Engineering. Shortly after enrolling, they started drafting college students but gave an exemption if you were married. I got married in 1960, so once again, I was exempt. Later they began to draft married men but you were exempt if you had children. My first child was born in 1962. Again I was exempt. I didn't consciously plan my life around this scenario but my actions did keep me from going to war and risking my life for an unjust cause.

We are now trading with our former enemy and the lives of the Vietnamese have dramatically improved since we left in defeat. I now believe that **it was a war not to be won,** but merely "sustained" for political and economic reasons. It has been reported that approximately 1.4 million military personnel were killed and 6% of those were members of the United States military. (84,000) In addition, it is estimated that there were 2 million civilian casualties. I no longer feel guilty for not coming to the aid of my country to participate in the killing of 3.4 million people for nothing more than a flawed military policy brought about by our government.

Ron Paul's book, *Freedom Under Siege*, says on page 76, "...But conscription is not authorized by the Constitution, either explicitly or implicitly. Neither Congress nor the president has the authority to draft or register anyone."

A compulsory draft is not only unconstitutional but also unfair and uneconomical. In my case cited above, should I have been given an exemption because I was attending college or had children? Why was my life more important than someone not attending college? Do you actually think that a draftee will fight as well as a professional soldier? What about the cost of training a draftee verses a career soldier?

If our foreign policies followed the Constitution we would not go to war unless we were attacked. If the United States of America was attacked, you wouldn't need a draft at all since most every man, woman and child old enough to fire a weapon would volunteer to protect their country. You only need to **force** a draft upon the American people when you are fighting someone else's war or are meddling in the affairs of other countries to protect our oil interests or make a profit for the international bankers and military industrial complex companies.

I would gladly risk dying for my country if the United States were attacked, but not for any other reason. If I had children of military age today, I would encourage them to not enlist in the military unless it was absolutely necessary to defend America. It looks like the Viet Nam protestors of the 1960's were correct after all. I don't see the situation in Iraq and Afghanistan today as being any different.

Some would say that, the 9-11 attack justified the U.S. attack on Iraq. This would have been true if Saddam Hussein was involved in the 9-11 attack . Besides shouldn't we have attacked Saudi Arabia since most of the 19 alleged hijackers were from there?

Define your terms- *When someone labels you as "Anti-Semitic", aren't they implying that you want to wipe Israel off the face of the earth, kill all the Jews in the world and that you deny the Holocaust occurred? This seems to be the common definition. This may be their definition but not necessarily yours.*

It may be that you are merely criticizing the actions of the Zionist Israeli government. ***Shouldn't that be allowed without you being unfairly labeled anti-Semitic?***

Why is it wrong for a Gentile to be Anti-Semitic to those Jews who are Anti-Gentile? Is the preceding statement anti-Semitic or is it a legitimate observation?

A person who criticizes President George Bush and Vice President Dick Cheney's actions are not considered "Anti-American" or "Anti –Christian." They simply disagree with the administration's policies.

Chapter Ten
Anti-Semitism

Once I was unjustly accused of being anti-Semitic by a local Jewish politician who had read an article I had written to the editor of one of our local newspapers criticizing Israel's Zionist government. He was very adept in using the old tried and effective method of attacking his opponent by labeling them "anti-Semitic." He didn't realize that I understood this technique and that it **would not** silence nor intimidate me. This was quite an insult since I knew that I wasn't anti-Semitic; at least according to my definition.

My definition of Anti-Semitism is when a person believes that all Jews should be killed, or the Holocaust never happened or that the state of Israel should be wiped off the face of the earth. I certainly don't believe the Jewish people should be harmed in any way. Just because I don't support the actions of the Zionist government of Israel, I should not be labeled anti-Semitic. I don't support all of President Obama's policies but don't consider myself anti-American or anti-Christian. I oppose many Israeli Zionist policies but that does not mean I dislike the Jewish people. I like and respect most Jewish people as long as they are **not** part of the Zionist movement and that they do not take literally the Talmud's view on how Jews are to treat non-Jews. In fact there are many orthodox Jews that don't support the Zionist government of Israel and they are not labeled anti-Semitic.

I understand that the Jewish Talmud says that Jews are not to have a country of their own, called Israel, until the coming of their messiah, which hasn't happened yet. In the meantime they are to live in their host country and respect the laws of that country. It appears to me that the Zionist Israeli government has hijacked the Jewish religion, distorting its true message, resulting in a great deal of bloodshed and hardships in the Middle East and for that matter the entire world. How much longer will we have to suffer because of the "Zionists" flawed ideology?

Global Anti-Semitic Review Act of 2004

Few American citizens are aware that on October 16, 2004 President Bush signed into law the **Global Anti-Semitic Review Act.** On May 22, 2006 Condoleezza Rice swore in Gregg Rickman to head up the Office of Global Anti-Semitism. Following is a summary of their definition of Anti-Semitism:

- Any assertion that the Jewish community controls government, the media, and international business and finance.
- Strong anti-Israel sentiment.
- Virulent criticism of Israel's leaders, past or present.
- Criticism of the Jewish religion or its religious leaders or literature (Including the Talmud and the Kabala)
- Criticism of the U.S. government and Congress for being under undue influence by the Jewish Zionist community.
- Criticism of the Jewish community for promoting globalism. (Sometimes referred to as the New World Order)
- Blaming Jewish leaders and their followers for inciting the Crucifixion of Jesus.
- Questioning the 6 million holocaust figure.
- Asserting that there is a Zionist Conspiracy.
- Claiming that Jews and their leaders created the Bolshevik revolution in Russia.
- Making derogatory statements about Jewish persons.

I keep asking myself, "What is the real motive behind this Act"? Also I question if this type of "Hate" legislation is even constitutional. I guess that it doesn't really matter with Dictators like Bush and Obama governing our country with 'Executive Orders' and completely disregarding our Constitution.

This Anti-Semitism Act signed into law by our President should sound off alarm bells throughout the nation. However, most Americans are not even aware that it was passed. I don't remember hearing about this on any newscast or reading about it in any of the newspapers. This Act scares the hell out of me! Just think what the consequences might be?

I guess it is now against the law to criticize any of the Jewish leaders. You cannot write about Meacham Begin's participation in the murderous terrorist movement cited by the British at the end of World War ll. You can't mention the massacre of Palestinian refugees in Sabra and Shatila under the leadership of Ariel Sharon. Winston Churchill's remarks about the Jewish involvement in the Bolshevik Russian Revolution will have to be stricken from the history books. Any person questioning the statistics of the holocaust is considered anti-Semitic and is subject to imprisonment and fines in several European countries. When will we begin to imprison Americans for breaking the Anti-Semitism Act?

Questioning the Holocaust
(Holocaust Revisionists or Holocaust Deniers)

The May/June 2008 issue of "The Barnes Review" has an interesting article written by Giuseppe Furioso entitled, "Outspoken Italian Revisionist Recounts 28 Problems He Has With the "Holocaust Legend". He explains that the Jewish "Holocaust" consists of three basic elements: (1) Approximately 6 million Jews were deliberately killed; (2) these killings were part of a state sponsored program on the part of the Third Reich, whose ultimate goal was the total eradication of the Jewish people; (3) the bulk of these murders took place in special "death camps" where the principal mechanism of execution was the homicidal gas chambers..... The author claims that he has no doubt that it actually could have happen-but certainly not in the ways that have been described thus far in the "official" literature. Following are paraphrased some of the problems the author has with the "Holocaust" story.

(1) If it were the Third Reich's intention to murder every Jew, why are there more than a million survivors today?

(Authors Comment: It appears that the Nazis murdered mainly those Jews that were too sick to work or did not have the mental capacity to work. Also many were killed as part of medical experiments)

(2) Giuseppe Furioso asks the question, "Why is there no mention of the 'Holocaust' in Churchill's six-volume *History of the Second World War,* the wartime memoirs of de Gaulle, Eisenhower's or any of the other luminaries who write about World War ll" ?

(3) "What were an inmate infirmary and a brothel doing in Auschwitz if in fact it was a death camp?"

(4) Why were the Jews taken hundreds of miles to a death camp to execute them? Why wouldn't they have killed them on the spot?

(5) Why haven't historians been able to come up with a single German document that point to a holocaust?

(6) It is still insisted that 6 million Jews died in the "Holocaust" even when the Auschwitz death toll has been reduced from 4 million to a figure less than a million.

Authors comment: Shouldn't the 6 million figure be revised to 3 million? Three million is still deplorable but since the adjustment has not been made, it makes one wonder what other facts need to be revised.

(7) The decoding of Germany's war time messages make no mention of mass executions........

(8) "The water table at Auschwitz lies a mere 18 inches below the surface, which makes claims of huge burning pits for the disposal of tens of thousands of victims untenable."

(9) If Zyklon B and hydrogen cyanide gas were used to execute the prisoners, how was it that the prison personnel could enter the gas chambers after 20 minutes without any protective gear?

(10) "Why do we no longer hear claims that the Germans manufactured soap, lamp shades, and riding britches from the bodies of dead Jews? Could it be that in the light of modern forensic and DNA knowledge these claims are totally untenable?"

The author, Giuseppe Furioso, was very bold to have made these claims because "Holocaust Revisionism" has been criminalized in at least 16 countries. Under the **2004 American Global Anti-**

Semitic Review Act's definition of Anti-Semitism, millions of Americans could be classified as Anti-Semites for criticizing Israel and could be considered "domestic terrorists." Could they then be prosecuted under the Homeland Security Act and be sent to prison like in Europe? This is a scary thought in a country such as ours where the First Amendment to our Constitution supposedly guarantees us freedom of speech.

The newspaper, The American Free Press, says that the State Departments "Office of Global Anti-Semitism" says the New Testament claim that the Jews had Christ crucified is classical Anti-Semitism.

Also don't forget that Mel Gibson's movie, "The Passion of The Christ" shows that Jewish leaders incited a Jewish mob and persuaded Pilate to have Christ crucified. I guess that Mel Gibson could be imprisoned sometime in the future for violating the Anti-Semitism Act. This is an example of just how serious the Anti-Semitism law has become. Millions of good people around the world are now going to be classified as anti-Semitic and in some parts of the world are being put in prison for their views. It is just a matter of time before Americans will be imprisoned for expressing their views about the Holocaust or criticizing Israel.

Actually, the issue asserting that the New Testament is Anti-Semitic is ridiculous. Especially if you believe as I do that the Biblical Christ was a mythical person- **no one** was killed. The true historical Christ is believed by some scholars to **not have been** crucified and did not die until several years later. Where would the Christian faith be today if the real Jesus Christ **had not** died on the cross? Christianity would not even exist in its present form today.

If our government and the Jews claim that the New Testament is an example of Anti-Semitism then the Jewish Talmud and the Old Testament are certainly examples of **"Anti-Gentilism."** Refer to chapter Four to see how the Talmud speaks of hatred towards the gentiles. Even though it isn't politically correct, shouldn't we allow this criticism go both ways?

Maybe **both** the Jewish Talmud and Christian Bible need to be revised, omitting all the superstitious and mythological drivel; the only problem, there wouldn't be much left. Until the religious ideology is changed and the believers understand and accept the truth, we will continue to experience problems between the various belief systems.

After reading what I have written about the Jewish religion and the Zionist government of Israel, I sincerely hope that the reader does not label me unjustly as, "Anti-Semitic." I am not! When you are reading or discussing the issues surrounding Israel, be sure to make a distinction between the views of the Jewish people and those of the Israeli Zionist government.

Also keep in mind that many of the "confessions" of German war criminals at the Nuremberg trials concerning the atrocities against the Jews were coerced with torture. Other Nazis, like Werner Von Braun who was instrumental in killing many people in Britain with rocket attacks, were not punished at all but rather given permission to enter the United States to work on our space program.

Keeping the Holocaust in Perspective

Yes, the Holocaust did happen, but, apparently not exactly like the historians have portrayed it. The estimated, and most likely exaggerated six million Jews that supposedly were killed, may need to be revised downward; plus you need to put all the statistics in the proper prospective to adequately understand all the pain and suffering experienced by other groups as well. Wasn't 6 million Jews also claimed to have been killed or persecuted in WWI? I doubt that we can ever be certain the exact number of Jews killed by Hitler. How much longer does the rest of the world have to suffer because of this terrible incident in history? The thing to learn from this horrifying event is to not ever allow it to happen again.

It makes me very uncomfortable to view the hundreds of pictures of dead and starving prisoners taken in the German prison camps at the end of the war. However one must realize that not all the prisoners shown in the pictures were Jews; many were Russian and other groups of political prisoners. Also near the end of the war, the Allies had cut off so many supply lines that both the German people and the prisoners were in short supply of food. It would only take a few months for the health conditions to deteriorate to the starvation point. With all the chaos of the bombing raids, the prisoners were pretty well neglected. I don't believe these extreme conditions existed until close to the end of the war.

The Soviet Army had systematically murdered 14,000 Polish officers in the Katyn Forest which some historians believe later became the inspiration for the false stories of columns of Jews being marched into rural areas and executed.

It has been estimated that **80 million** "goyim" (an offensive Jewish term for people who are not Jewish) were exterminated in Russia by mainly a Jewish political regime. Some of the executioners bore the names of Firine Kaganovitch, Yagoda, Frenkel, Jejoff, Ourenski, Rappaport and other Jewish names.

Why doesn't anyone talk about this atrocity against the gentiles? If these facts are true, wouldn't we have an example here of an "anti-Gentilism Holocaust?"

The firestorm incineration of German civilians from the bombing by the Allies, the hundreds of thousands of Japanese civilians bombed in Hiroshima and Nagasaki, the murder of one million anti-communist Russians whom Eisenhower handed over to Soviet executioners, the millions of Chinese murdered by the Japanese, the thousands of Allied soldiers that died and many other horrors puts the "6 Million" purported deaths in the Jewish "Holocaust" in perspective. The Jews were not the only ones to suffer during this era of WWl and WWll. In many cases the Zionist Jews were at least partially responsible for their own suffering and they themselves were responsible for the killing of thousands of gentiles in Russia.

The question now is, whom do you believe has truthfully recorded the events of the "Holocaust"- the historians and Jewish sources or the historical investigators called "Revisionists?" It is very difficult to give up old belief systems that have been engrained into you for over 60 years. But when one examines the facts, it is obvious we have been lied to about many details of the Holocaust. This important issue definitely warrants further study without fear of being labeled "Anti-Semitic".

Greater Israel

The hidden controllers start and stoke conflicts and wars for huge profits and for global control. One example is their getting the Jews and Muslims to kill each other. (With the assistance of the United States) One of **Israel's** goals in these conflicts is the creation of a Greater Israel.

Over the years the United States has supported Israel with billions of dollars in money and arms which has been a huge waste of the tax payer's money. Israel's continued immoral and brutal agenda of expansion should not be supported by the U.S. **Of course** the Palestinians resist Israeli aggression and naturally fight back. Should the Palestinians be called "Terrorists" or "Freedom Fighters"? With Israel's agenda of adding additional territory to their country, there will never be peace in the Middle East until they have vacated the Gaza strip and the West Bank. Any further settlements (colonization) must be halted if we are ever to have peace in the Middle East.

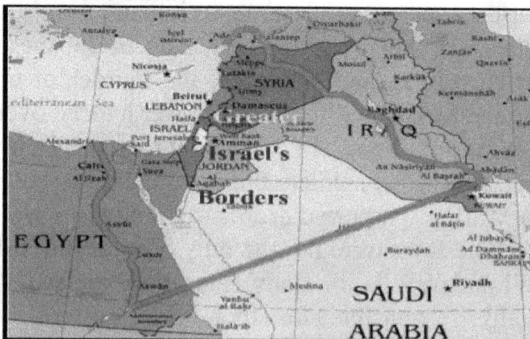

**(Genesis Biblical Reference) -Within the red outline-
Nile River to the Euphrates**

Three Definitions of the Term "Greater Israel"

(1) The current territory of the State of Israel including the Palestinian territories.

(2) The territory of the former British mandate of Palestine, either in the 1923 or 1948 borders.

(3) Biblical ref.: Genesis 15: 18-21, Numbers 34: 1-15, and Ezekiel 47: 13-20.

Genesis

Includes territory from the Nile to the Euphrates. It vaguely includes all of modern day Israel, the Palestinian territories, Lebanon, large parts of Syria, Jordan and Egypt. It is debatable as to whether it includes a portion of current Iraq, Saudi Arabia and Turkey. (reference map above)

Numbers and Ezekiel

A much smaller territory is described in these two passages.

No matter which definition you wish to use, the fact is that Israel's long term plan is to expand its territory and rule the entire world. There were 285,000 Israeli settlements in the Palestinian West bank as of 2008. They cleverly use the term "settlements" which is in reality classical "Colonization" that has been used to acquire new territory for centuries; same as what England, France, and Spain's colonies attempted to do in what is now the United States. All the peace agreement talks are about Israel halting construction of settlements on Palestinian land. If Israel was serious about peace, they would be talking about **abandoning** these settlements?

Israel **used** the United States to overthrow Iraq so they could re-establish themselves there plus to remove any threat from Saddam Hussein. What will the Jews' **return** to Iraq be called?

"Settlements", "Colonization" or will they claim they are merely returning home. Currently Iraq is resisting the immigration of the Israelis fearing that the problems of the Zionist movement will be added to their country more than it has already.

Israel does not need to be concerned about having "settlements" in the United States to expand its territory here. They already control our government through the various lobbying groups, banking institutions, telecommunication companies, entertainment industry and they control a large portion of the major news media. Israel's own media alludes to this. Prime Minister Ariel Sharon has been quoted as saying to foreign minister Sharon Peres: "Don't worry about American pressure; we control America". Some in America sarcastically state that Israel may as well become our 51st state.

A recent joke circulating on the internet states that the U.S. offered to make Israel our 51st state. Israel stated that then they would only have two senators so must decline the offer. Currently the Israeli lobby controls most of our Senate **and** House of Representatives.

Note: It has been argued whether the two blue bars on the Israeli flag represent the territory between the Nile in Egypt and Tigris Euphrates rivers in Iraq. Could it be that it is Israel's long term goal to include this area as part of a Greater Israel?'

Chapter Eleven
Subliminal Warfare

John Perkins book, *"Confessions of an Economic Hit Man"* describes a new type of warfare that doesn't require the firing of a single shot to take control of another country. Before reading his excellent book, I had suspected this type of clandestine operation might be taking place but couldn't quite put all the pieces together.

The author explains that he got a job early in his career working for a large consulting firm that did work in developing third world countries. It was his job to do a feasibility study for the United States Government, the host country, the international bankers and the construction companies like Halliburton and Bechtel. He was encouraged to make the analysis justify the spending of billions of dollars for such projects as hydroelectric plants, state of the art communication systems, etc. It was more important for the project to be approved than insuring that the huge loan could be paid back. In fact some were designed in such a way that it would be almost impossible for the small country to ever pay back the loan, especially in cash.

Just as planned, many times the host country could not meet their obligations to pay back the loan. In some cases our government would agree to reduce the loan or even forgive the entire loan if the United States could get the country to support the U.S. vote in the United Nations, grant land for military bases in that country or allow us to take over operation or control of their natural resources. All of this without firing a shot! Everyone was a winner except the poor peasants of the third world country and the American taxpayer. The U.S. government got what it wanted, the bankers made millions on interest payments, companies like Halliburton and Bechtel made millions of dollars for their stockholders, and the leaders and their relatives of this third world country gained immense wealth. In most cases the peasants were worse off than before, and the American tax payer got fleeced.

This is a much cheaper and more efficient means of gaining control of another country than going to war. If someone blows the whistle and exposes what is taking place, our government can blame the consulting firm or contracting companies. If this economic assistance plan doesn't work, the CIA might possibly assassinate the leader of the country (i.e. Panama and Ecuador?) or spend a few million dollars to aid the leader's opponent and set up a puppet government favorable to U.S. policies. Remember how the U.S. installed the Shah of Iran in 1953 by orchestrating the overthrow of Iran's popular Prime Minister, Mohammed Mossadegh? (Not a very good way to make friends and influence people.)

If we had adhered to the Constitution as our founding fathers planned, this type of unethical foreign policy would not have taken place. George Washington's 1796 Farewell Address advised us to avoid, "foreign entanglements." The advice of these former great leaders of our country is gradually and systematically being ignored.

Intellectual growth should commence at birth and cease only at death.
Albert Einstein

Chapter Twelve
What Can You Do?

Most people think that just voting for their favorite candidate is good enough. Some think they must follow the party line no matter who the National Convention Party leaders select. Perhaps their father and grandfather were Republicans and that was good enough for them. Joe Blow could run on the republican ticket and they would vote for him; he must be a good candidate, the National Convention chose him! There is really no need to vote at all if this is how shallow your thinking is regarding politics.

Getting Informed and Involved

Getting informed about the political issues is not that difficult. Watching the six o'clock news and reading only one local newspaper does not give you enough information to properly assess the important issues. In addition you must read books about the politicians and issues, research issues on the internet, attend political rallies, personally meet the candidates and join one of your local political parties. Consider running for a committeeman or committeewoman of your local voting precinct so you can have some input as to the national party platform that will be adopted. You may even want to become a delegate or run for political office. Also be sure to talk to your friends about the important subjects presented in this book and encourage the political candidates in your area to adopt a platform that you feel is important. The important thing is to get informed and then get involved.

An Appeal to the American Public to Take Back their Country

Almost everyone we meet these days will gladly give their opinion as to why our country is in so much trouble. However, most of the public's information that forms their opinions is received from the biased controlled mainstream news media. The media continually reports the same distorted news over and over as expounded by the special interest groups and those with selfish hidden agendas.

One will hear that subprime mortgages, the deregulation of Wall Street, the energy shortage, global warming, cost of fighting terrorism, etc. are the culprits. None can deny that these issues contribute to the cause of our economic problems; however, almost no one discusses the **real** reasons why our country is in so much trouble.

The real issue is that our present form of government, a "Democracy" and its monetary policies are flawed. Given enough time our existing monetary policies are destined to fail. Government intervention, with its trillion dollar bailouts only delays the total failure. These huge bailouts with almost unlimited credit and cash infusion, with "phony" money, which we don't even have, will only make things worse in the end. This type of irresponsible government intervention got us into this mess in the first place. The best thing our government could do is **nothing** and let these inefficient and sometime corrupt businesses fail.

A TV news reporter asked her guest if he believed the "Economic Stimulus" plan was going to work. The guest said, *"Absolutely!"* *"It will increase the debt and will increase the size of our government."* I thought, *"Wow, this guy hit the nail on the head."* Not expecting such an honest answer the reporter immediately changed the subject so as not to deviate from the TV networks preconceived agenda. Why won't the controlled media and our elected representatives talk about the real issues, and openly discuss that it just might be that our Federal Reserve banking system is not working and should be abolished? The answer is obvious. The elite bankers are so powerful and wealthy that they have purchased control of all the major media. And of course they hide their elicit deeds through the use of their propaganda disseminated by the media.

Our wise founding fathers warned us of the dangers of a private banking system and a controlled press. If one will recall, the pledge of allegiance to our flag still says, "I pledge allegiance to the flag of the United States of America and to the **Republic** for which it stands… (Not to the **Democracy** for which it stands.) Our

128

founding fathers looked upon a "Democracy" in contempt. In fact, the word "Democracy" does not even appear in the Declaration of Independence or the Constitution. A "Democracy" form of government sounds good until you understand all the ramifications connected to it. Democracy is actually "Mob Rule" where 51% can vote and decide that the other 49% have no representation. Thus the citizens of a Democracy will continue to elect those leaders who promise to provide them with all the necessities of life through social welfare--by redistributing the wealth. Eventually the hand outs will be so great that the working class **(producers)** will no longer be willing or able to support the non working or retired **(consumer)** class. Therefore, this system by its very design, must eventually fail. It is only a matter of time. In a Republic, however, everyone (100%) is represented by the Constitution and a court system administered by or ruled by just laws and a small federal government that respects the sovereignty of the individual states.

Note this simple example that explains the difference between a **Republic** and a **Democracy** when someone is accused of committing a crime:

Democracy--When a group of 10 cowboys, each wearing black hats and armed to the teeth, after pursuing and apprehending a suspected, low down horse thief, also wearing a black hat, vote 6 to 4 to hang him. Before they can hang him, the sheriff, sporting a spotless white Stetson, rides up and casually says, **Republic--** "Stop fellas, I am taking this man back to town to be tried in a court of law by a jury of his peers. If he is found guilty we will hang him. If he is found innocent, we will celebrate and invite the whole town to a picnic."

Which form of government would you prefer if you were suspected of, accused of, and arrested for an alleged crime?

Most of our economic problems today began with the adoption of a private central banking system. One of the greatest crimes ever perpetrated against this country was the Federal Reserve Act passed in 1913, an act authorizing, once again, a **private bank** to print the United States currency and then charge our government (taxpayers) interest on our own money. Also in 1913, the 16th Amendment allowed our government to collect income tax on people's salaries in order to pay the interest the <u>private</u> Federal Reserve charges us.

The only politicians, with any common sense, that I have heard talking about this issue is Congressman Ron Paul from Texas and Congressman Dennis Kucinich from Ohio. Dr. Paul, a physician, receives little exposure when he discusses this issue. Moreover, most of the controlled mainstream media went out of their way to marginalize him in the 2008 presidential election. This issue-- the promise to abolish the Federal Reserve--, was the main reason for the "controllers" to do whatever it took to keep Congressman Paul from being elected president. Had congressman Paul been successful, his rational policies would not only have cost the "Banksters" billions of dollars of ill gained profits, but would have severely limited their stranglehold on the American banking system, economy, and the so called "free enterprise system." The Federal Reserve banking system is extremely beneficial to the "Banksters" but particularly detrimental to the American people since under this system our government can never pay off the national debt.

To have sound monetary policies in this country, we, the people-the true government must (1) **abolish** the Federal Reserve, (2) **abolish** the fractional reserve banking which allows banks to create money out of thin air by loaning up to 9 to 10 times more money than they have on deposit and (3) **abolish** income tax on people's salaries.

Think for a moment how you could stimulate, not only the economy but improve your personal well-being if you were not required to pay personal income tax on your wages. A tax on your wages is a form of slavery. Where is the profit? All you have done is to trade your labor (sweat) for money. The government is forcing you to work a portion of your work day for free.

Contrary to popular belief our monetary system does not need and never has needed to be backed by gold or silver. (Except to be constitutional) Granted, precious metal backing could limit the amount of paper money put into circulation and help keep inflation under control, but the same thing can be accomplished by tying the amount of money to be printed to the yearly increase in our country's Gross Domestic Product. (GDP) In this way the money is backed by sweat (value added) and an increase in production. This "value added" plus our government's acceptance of this paper money for the payment of taxes is all that is need for backing.

Power-hungry presidents like George W. Bush completely ignored the Constitution and disregarded the will of the people by going to war without proper congressional approval. Essentially ruling like a tyrannical dictator, he used "Executive Orders" (expanded Executive "Privilege") and overlooked the "War Powers Resolutions" of 1973 which curbed the president's power to commit armed forces to hostilities abroad without congressional approval. It also requires that the president notify congress within 48 hours of committing armed forces to military action and forbids armed forces from remaining for more than 60 days without an authorization of the use of military force or a declaration of war.

In addition President Bush lied to us about (1) Weapons of Mass Destruction, (2) the true perpetrators of the 9-11 attack, (3) the justification for the "Patriot Act", (4) energy shortages and (5) man made global warming. Over the last several years the Executive Branch has destroyed the "checks and balances" of a sound government while the Legislative and the Judiciary allowed this wrongful seizure of sovereignty belonging to "the People."

Were you aware that in most wars the same **international bankers** finance **both sides** of the conflict? If you do not believe this, I encourage you to do some research to see who financed the Bolshevik Revolution and the Allied and Axis powers during World War I and World War II. Now, compare the foreign policy of the United States today that continues to give billions of dollars and state of the art military equipment each year to Israel and also money to the Palestinians. When will this insanity and inhumanity end?

In many countries of Europe today any remarks or criticism about Israel or questioning the details of the "Holocaust" could land you in jail. Moreover if the United States **Global Anti-Semitic Review Act of 2004** were enforced in this country, the same thing could happen here. Due to the news media's silence on this issue most people don't even know that this act exists, or how serious of a threat it is to our constitutional rights of "Freedom of Speech."

This book you are now reading, *"Secrets of our Hidden Controllers Revealed"* elaborates on the important issues facing us today and hopefully will encourage you to begin researching these issues in order that you will be in a better position to elect those politicians that will make the necessary changes to once again make this the greatest country in the world.

Following is a synopsis- a non-partisan political platform that all citizens of this country, regardless of political party affiliation- should encourage their representatives to adopt. We can make a difference, but only if enough of us become better informed on the important issues and begin electing those politicians who will make the changes necessary to return our country to that which our founding fathers intended.

Proposed Non-Partisan Political Platform

(1) Abolish the private and unconstitutional Federal Reserve System, fractional reserve banking and income taxes on people's salaries.

(2) Stop meddling in the affairs of other nations. Bring our troops home immediately from Iraq, Afghanistan and the other military bases throughout the world because modern weapons and delivery systems make these bases obsolete. If we want to destroy our country like the Romans did, then we can continue pursuing the policy of preemptive strikes and our attempting to police the world.

(3) Uphold the Constitution by taking the power of declaring war away from the president and require Congress to approve all declarations of war, as provided for in our Constitution. The power to declare war is too much power for one person.

(4) Enact legislation to limit the influence of the thousands of lobbyists, by disallowing all former members of Congress and their staff, all former members of the Executive Branch and their staff, and all former judges at the Federal level and their staff from becoming lobbyists within ten years of their government service. Any individual that violates this statute will be prosecuted, fined and face possible imprisonment.

(5) Adopt a single subject Federal Law, similar to Missouri law, for all bills before Congress. No bill may contain more than one subject, which is to be expressed clearly in its title. This alone would eliminate the thousands of "ear mark" (pork) provisions attached to almost all the bills before Congress. The argument about whether the president should have the line item veto power would no longer be relevant. The simplicity of bills under this change would make it much easier for our representatives to vote intelligently, and the American public might even be able to understand the bills. The cost savings alone to the American tax payers would be enormous.

(6) Require presidential "Executive Orders" to be reviewed and approved or denied by Congress. There may need to be exceptions to this rule regarding national security issues.

(7) Abolish unfair "Free Trade" agreements such as NAFTA, CAFTA, GATT that send our jobs overseas. Adopt **Fair Trade** polices instead of **Free Trade** disasters.

(8) Abolish the "Patriot Act." (More accurately the Un Patriotic Act) The Patriot Act is more about taking away our freedoms than it is fighting terrorism.

(9) Require judges to inform jurors of their constitutional right to declare a law as unjust and not applicable to a particular case and that they can find a defendant **"not guilty"** for any reason. This is the final defense that Americans have from a possible tyrannical government or biased judge.

(10) Decriminalize the use of marijuana, cocaine and heroin and make these drugs available at a reasonable cost only to someone that has had a blood test that shows they are already addicted. We could then treat these "sick" individuals, rich and poor, and offer treatment rather than classifying them as criminals and institutionalizing them at a great cost to the taxpayer. The savings from not institutionalizing an addict would go a long way in paying for their treatment.

The benefits?

(a) No longer would these addicts need to commit crimes to support their habit.
(b) Taxpayers would save billions of dollars.
(c) It would remove the incentive to produce illicit drugs and eliminate all drug profits from terrorist organizations and rogue elements within our CIA that use drug profits to finance their clandestine operations.
(d) It would lessen the investment of illicit drug profits that artificially support Wall Street investments.
(e) One could then identify the real criminals.

There are only two ways to win "The War on Drugs;" (1) Convince all addicts and recreational users to stop-which isn't going to happen and (2) Make these drugs legal and treat users as "sick" and assist them in breaking the habit. Drugs like "Meth" **should not** be legalized.

This very controversial issue must be addressed and new solutions found so that we can once and for all win the **"War on Drugs"** before it destroys the entire world. The violence connected to the drug traffickers is now spreading to the United States. Cities like Phoenix, Arizona have had a huge increase in drug related crimes including beheadings, executions and kidnappings. What we are currently doing to win the "War On Drugs" isn't working and never will.

(11) Adopt a constitutional amendment establishing Congressional term limits. (12 years maximum) In order to assure that this measure would pass, it would be necessary to exempt the current representatives as long as they were continually re-elected.

We would be better represented by short term representatives than life long professional politicians that are more easily controlled by the lobbyists.

(12) Prohibit the military industrial complex companies, the elite banking interests, the oil companies, and the Israeli lobby from dictating the United States foreign policy.

(13) Revise high school and college text books to include honest discussions of the Federal Reserve Banking System, fractional reserve banking, the origin of money, the history of the House of Rothschild banking interests and the part that Wall Street investment groups like the Carlyle Group, Goldman Sachs and Blackstone have on our country's monetary and foreign policies.

Include discussions of the "Council on Foreign Relations", the "Bilderbergers", The "Trilateral Commission" and the "International Monetary Fund." Explain how members of these groups, which, by the way, are not elected, control the domestic and foreign policies of this country.

Explain the difference between a "Republic" form of government and a "Democracy" form of government. In 1787 at the close of the Constitutional Convention in Philadelphia, a woman asked Benjamin Franklin what kind of government had just been set up. He replied, "A Republic if you can keep it." It looks like Benjamin Franklin's concerns were correct. We weren't able to keep it.

Hopefully, some of our bright young students being taught the **truth** about our country's history will become future leaders and save us from a tyrannical federal government.

(14) Require corporations to allow their stockholders (excluding the CEO and Directors) to determine the salaries and bonuses of their CEO's and directors.

(15) Pass legislation that makes it illegal for Wall Street investment companies to engage in "Las Vegas type investments" (gambling) such as derivatives and unnecessary commodity trading. Do not reward these companies with "bailouts" by giving them our tax money to reimburse them for their criminal activity, huge bonuses and poor management decisions.

(16) Do not allow the federal government to get involved in local law enforcement.

(17) The state National Guard is to protect the individual states—not police the world.

<u>Repeal</u> the Montgomery Amendment to the National Defense Authorization Act for 1987. This act states that a governor **cannot** withhold consent with regard to active duty outside the United States because of any objection to the location, purpose, type, or schedule of such duty. This unconstitutional law was challenged but was upheld by the Supreme Court—*Perpich v. Department of Defense*, 496 U.S. *334 (1990)* As part of our "Checks and Balance" system, each state's governor should be in charged of when and where its own National Guard units will be deployed.

(18) Repeal the **Global Anti-Semitic Review Act of 2004** that makes it illegal to criticize the country of Israel or individual Jews.

(19) Learn to make use of "Initiatives" and Referendums" (ballot measures or propositions) at the state level if your legislature fails to act in a responsible way.

Note: Prepare your own platform list and then pressure your representatives to make the necessary changes to cure our ailing nation. Make it clear that you intend to vote for only those candidates who support the majority of these issues.

Don't be tricked by those who want you to believe that this is a battle between the Democrats' and the Republicans' ideologies. Regardless of your party affiliation, these are the issues that will continue to affect you, your children, your grandchildren, great grandchildren, and even their children. It is imperative that you address these issues and be a part of the movement for real change.

In Conclusion

The American people elect only 536 people to run our country- 1 President, 100 Senators, and 435 Congressmen.

These representatives are the ones primarily responsible for all the domestic problems facing us today. Have you ever wondered how this small group of politicians could claim that they are against (1) high taxes, (2) deficit spending, (3) operating the government without a balanced budget, (4) policies that cause inflation, and (5) constant wars or "Regime Change" as they like to refer to them. How can they explain that we still have all these problems if they are against the policies that cause them? Every four years the politicians who created the problems promise to fix them but seldom do they make much progress. They will lie and argue that there are strange unknown forces that affect our economy and cause inflation. They simply will not admit that they allow the elite bankers and lobbyists to persuade them to vote in favor of agendas that are not in the best interests of the American people.

As stated earlier in this book, the elite bankers are the "Controllers Behind the Curtain" or the "Shadow Government" that manipulate our 536 elected officials to implement their own personal agendas. But don't forget that the Congress that voted for and passed the law that established the unconstitutional Federal Reserve Act in 1913 is the same branch of government that can abolish it today.

Keep in mind that our monetary system must be controlled by the **U.S. Government** as provided for in the Constitution and not by a **private bank** that has been licensed to counterfeit money and to engage in "fractional reserve banking." The Federal Reserve System has stolen literally trillions of dollars from us citizens over the years.

The Federal Reserve and income taxes on the citizen's wages must be abolished. Also contrary to popular belief, our money does not need to be backed by gold or silver. The colonies did just fine in 1776 with no precious metal backing. (The United States did not have any significant amount of gold until the 1849 gold rush) The fact that our government will accept the paper money as payment of taxes and the value added by a person's labor is all that is needed for backing. Granted, having the money supply backed by gold and silver would help insure that a **limited** amount of paper money would be issued which would in turn protect the existing money from being devalued by inflation. However, there are other means to limit the amount of paper money printed. The paper money supply must be just enough to conduct commerce; money backed by gold and silver would not provide the needed amount of money necessary for commerce to be conducted efficiently. As the economy grows, an equivalent amount of money must be issued. With the abolishment of the Federal Reserve, our nation can once again return to a debt free society. As long as we continue to pay interest to the Federal Reserve for them loaning us our own money, we cannot ever become debt free.

National Dividends to American Citizens

Richard C Cook, in his book entitled, "*We Hold These Truths- The Hope of Monetary Reform*" states that ..."But the income that is generated through wages, salaries, and dividends is never enough to consume the GDP, because a portion must be withheld (saved) as retained earnings for future investment. This is the "gap." The way society decides to fill this gap, reflects whether it views itself as an empire, where the rich profit at the expense of the many, or a democracy, where all members of society have the opportunity to prosper." ..."the author also stated that "according to his calculations derived from publically-available economic data for 2006, the government should have paid a $12,600 cash dividend that year, on average, to everyone in the U. S." Another term for this is described by C.H. Douglas as "Social Credit."

Wikipedia states that **"Social Credit** is described by its originator. H. Douglas (1879-1952). According to Douglas, the true purpose of *production* is *consumption*, and production must serve the genuine, freely expressed interests of consumers. Each citizen is to have a beneficial, not direct, inheritance in the communal capital conferred by complete and dynamic access to the fruits of industry assured by the National Dividend and Compensated Price.

Consumers, fully provided with adequate *purchasing power*, will establish the policy of *production* through exercise of their monetary vote.... Social Credit philosophy is best summed by Douglas when he said, Systems were made for men, and not men for systems, and the interest of man which is *self-development*, is above all systems, whether theological, political or economic."

For the elite controllers to maintain their influence on the world, they must keep the common people in a state of political antagonism. They will win if they can succeed in dividing the voters and get them to spend all of their energy in fighting over issues of little importance.

As you do your own investigation, formulate your own political platform and share it with your friends and political leaders. Sadly, you will probably find that many of them will not be interested or will not want to make an effort to discover the truth, but the effort must be made if "We the People" are to regain control of our government. Become aware of and informed about how your opinions are being controlled by the media, our educational system, the religious organizations and our own government. As more and more people get involved, our ailing Republic will once again become the great nation as envisioned by our wise founding fathers.

I see hope in that some of our state representatives have recognized the threat of our Federal Government gradually diminishing "States Rights." As of March 2009, 20 states have passed resolutions in defiance of the Federal Government's intrusion into states' rights. They have demanded that the Federal Government obey the Constitutions' 9th and 10th Amendments. It appears that the "controllers" do not have as much control over our state representatives as they do over our federal representatives.

If you believe that a "One World Government" or the "New World Order" is a good idea, just consider an example on a smaller scale. Think about our 50 states being dissolved and the Federal government governing all of us as one state. It is frightening to think what would happen to our civil rights and way of life and worse yet no way for the individual to ever get anything changed.

Earlier in this book, I stated that the changes that need to be made by our country must be made through our existing **two party** system, even though CNN's Lou Dobbs disagreed and was advising his viewers to register as an Independent. After seeing how the 2008 election was fraudulently handled by the controlled mass news media, the Federal, State, and county political organizations, it is now obvious to me that it may be necessary to make the needed changes through a **third party** or an actual revolution. It seems unlikely that the current leadership in both the Republican and Democrat parties will ever oppose the powerful lobbyists. It would be preferable to make the necessary changes through the existing Democrat and Republican parties but the "controllers" are too well entrenched.

I definitely do not support an armed revolution as a method of change but if things continue to deteriorate it will be the only alternative. Someone once said, "Our liberty is protected by four boxes- the ballot box, the jury box, the soap box and finally the cartridge box." Let's hope we don't have to use the cartridge box to make the changes.

It didn't really matter whether you voted for Barack Obama or John McCain in the 2008 presidential election. All the candidates except Congressman Ron Paul, Dennis Kucinich and Senator Mike Gravel were members of the Council on Foreign Relations. The CFR's stated goal is the dismantling of American sovereignty in order to bring about an all-powerful One World Government. When you voted for one of the front runners, you just **thought** you had a choice. The American people believe they **elect** their president when in reality, the elites behind the scenes **"selected"** the president.

Both Barack Obama and John McCain said they support change and the American people continue to fall for these empty promises by voting every four years for the same lies.

Albert Einstein once said, "Insanity is doing the same thing over and over and expecting different results".

When is this Insanity going to end?

Appendix
Bible References

More than three hundred years after the birth of Jesus Christ, the Catholic Council of Carthage in 397 AD selected the ancient books that were to be included in the Christian Bible. They picked and chose and edited those books to tell the story they wanted told- even if it wasn't the truth. Keep in mind that much Oral material was also included in the Bible. You know how accurate that can be if you ever participated in a party exercise where five or six people are lined up and a message is whispered into the ear of each person and relayed to the next. The message at the end usually doesn't resemble the original.

A few controversial passages, with the author's comments, have been selected here to assist the reader in determining if the Bible is in fact "Divinely Inspired."

There will be some that will claim that these examples have been taken out of context and don't necessarily mean what they appear to say. I agree but rather than explaining and analyzing each passage, which could fill another book, I will leave it up to the reader to do their own research so they can attempt to understand the true meaning of each passage. Good luck, discovering the true meaning of Bible messages is a daunting task.

There is a passage in Shakespeare that pretty well explains how difficult and dangerous it is to understand and put into the proper perspective, passages from the Bible. "The devil can cite Scripture for his purpose. An evil soul producing holy witness is like a villain with a smiling cheek, A goodly apple rotten at the heart. O, what a goodly outside falsehood hath!" ("The merchant of Venice" Act 1, Scene 3)

The following Bible quotations are definitely <u>not</u> the word of <u>my</u> God:

Genesis 19:4-8 A group of sexually depraved men called unto Lot, "Bring them out unto us that we may know them" (meaning Lots two male visitors) Lot says "Behold now, I have two daughters which have not known man...do ye to them as is good in your eyes".

Genesis 19:30 -38 Lot's daughters trick him into having sexual intercourse while he is drunk and both become pregnant.

Genesis 24:2-9, "... put, I pray thee, your hand under my thigh, and I will make thee swear by the Lord ...." (It was the custom at this time to put your hand under the testicles to take an oath. "Testament," "Testify," and "Testicle" are from the same root.)

Numbers 31:17-18 "Now therefore kill every male among the little ones, and kill every woman that hath known man by lying with him. But all the women children, that have not known a man by lying with him, keep alive for yourselves".

Deuteronomy 21:10-14, The Israelites are allowed to kidnap "beautiful women" with the Lord's approval from the enemy camp to be their trial wives. He can simply let her go if things don't work out.

II Kings 6:29 "So we boiled my son, and did eat him. And I said unto her on the next day, give thy son that we may eat him; and she hid her son". *Would you want this passage to be a part of your child's Bible study? How would you explain this to a child?*

II Kings 18:27, "... that they may eat their own dung and drink their own piss with you."

Isaiah 13:16 "Their children also shall be dashed to pieces before their eyes; their houses shall be spoiled, and their wives ravished."

Hosea 13:16 "They shall fall by the sword: their infants shall be dashed in pieces, and their women with child shall be ripped up."

Malachi 2:3 "Behold, I will corrupt your seed, and spread dung upon your faces..."

Genesis 6:11-17, God finds that the earth is corrupt and filled with violence. He decides to kill every living thing on the face of the earth other than Noah's family. *Pretty drastic measure!*

Exodus 12:29 The Lord kills all the first-born humans and first-born cattle in the land of Egypt.

Numbers 15:32-36 A man who gathered sticks for a fire on the Sabbath is stoned to death as the Lord commanded. *I guess we should close all hospitals, police departments and fire departments on the Sabbath as the lord commanded.*

Numbers 25:4 "And the Lord said unto Moses, take all the heads of the people, and hang them up before the Lord against the sun ...."

Numbers 31:31-40 32,000 virgins are taken by the Israelites as booty. Thirty-two are set aside (to be sacrificed?) as a tribute for the Lord.

Joshua 11:6 The Lord orders horses to be hamstrung. *What did the horse do to deserve this cruel treatment?*

ll Kings 15:16 Menahem ripped open all the women who were pregnant.

Ezekiel 9: 6 The Lord commands: "... slay old men outright, young men and maidens, little children and women ...."

Genesis 4:17 Cain builds and populates a whole city in only two generations. *Pretty remarkable!*

Genesis 7:17-19 the flood covered the entire earth at the same time. *There is no evidence of any world wide floods; only many local floods.*

Genesis 8:21 The odor of Noah's sacrifices was pleasing to the Lord. *What does this mean?*

Exodus 12:30 The Lord kills all the first-born of Egypt and there is not a house where there is not at least one dead. *This is very strange unlikely event!*

Isaiah 30:26 "Moreover the light of the moon shall be as the light of the sun, and the light of the sun shall be sevenfold..." *People used to believe that the moon and the planets were thought to give off their own light. You would think that God would have been aware of this.*

Genesis 3:16 Women should suffer pain during childbirth. *This verse was used by the Church to oppose the use of anesthesia during childbirth.)*

Genesis 15:18 Egypt, Jordan, Saudi Arabia, Lebanon, Syria, Yemen, and part of Iraq belong to the Jews only. *No wonder there will be no peace in the Middle East unless this Biblical scripture can be refuted.*

Exodus 20:4 We are not to make any graven images. *Does this include photographs, paintings, statues, etc? The Catholic Church might want to take inventory of their artwork!*

Exodus 21:15 "And he that smiteth his father or his mother will surely be put to death." *Pretty harsh treatment for a youngster!*

Exodus 22:29 Firstborn children should be sacrificed to the Lord.

Leviticus 20:13 Homosexuals are to be put to death. *I hope that there are not any Christians that believe this today. It will be really embarrassing to religious groups when science finally discovers that gays and lesbians are born that way and by no fault of their own, their plumbing doesn't match their sexuality.*

Deuteronomy 18:20-22, EZ 14:9 If a prophet's words do not come true, he is a false prophet and must be put to death. This is true even if he has been deceived by God himself.

Deuteronomy 23:2 A bastard--and his offspring to the tenth generation--are to be punished for his illegitimacy and cannot enter a congregation of the Lord. *This seems a little harsh!*

Deuteronomy 23:19-20 Money must not be lent at interest to a brother (meaning a fellow Israelite). Interest can only be collected from foreigners.

Mark 10:2-12, Luke 16:18 Divorce is wrong, and to remarry is to commit adultery.

Luke 14:26 One cannot be a disciple of Jesus unless he hates his mother, father, wife, children, brothers, sisters. *It seems like this requirement would weed out most normal people from becoming a disciple.*

1Corinthians 11:14 It is a shame for a man to have long hair. *Why is it, then, that most portrayals of Jesus show him with long hair?*

1Corinthians 14:34-35 Women are to be silent in church. If they have any questions, they are to ask their husbands at home. It is a shame for women to speak in church.

1Timothy 2:12 "But I suffer not a woman to teach, nor to usurp authority over the man, but to be in silence". *The Taliban sure believes this!*

Mathew 16:23 Jesus calls Peter [a] "Satan" and "a hindrance," and accuses him of being on the side of men rather than that of God. *Which is it? Is Peter really the first Pope as claimed by the Catholic Church?*

Deuteronomy 7:1 When the LORD thy God shall bring thee into the land whither thou goest to possess it, and hath cast out many nations before thee, the Hittites,...7:2 And when the LORD thy God shall deliver them before thee; thou shalt smite them, and utterly destroy them; thou shalt make no covenant with them, nor shew mercy unto them: ... 7:5 But thus shall ye deal with them; ye shall destroy their altars, and break down their images, and cut down their groves... 7:6 For thou art an holy people unto the LORD thy God: the LORD thy God hath chosen thee to be a special people unto himself, above all people that are upon the face of the earth. 7:16 And thou shalt consume all the people which the LORD thy God shall deliver thee; thine eye shall have no pity upon them: neither shalt thou serve their gods; for that will be a snare unto thee. 7:23 But the LORD thy God shall deliver them unto thee, and shall destroy them with a mighty destruction, until they be destroyed. 7:24 And he shall deliver their kings into thine hand, and thou shalt destroy their name from under heaven: there shall no man be able to stand before thee, until thou have destroyed them.

People who unjustly label non Jews as anti-Semitic for their views against Jews should read the Talmud and the Old Testament, particularly Deuteronomy-Chapter 7, to see how the Jews feel about non Jews. According to the Jewish Talmud, the non-Jew is considered an animal (beast) and has no property or legal rights. Many historical figures such as Voltaire, Thomas Jefferson, Henry Ford and even President Harry Truman have made comments on these abominable beliefs of the Jews.

Has the suffering of the Jews over the last 3,000 years been solely the unjust treatment of them by non Jews or has it been the consequences of how the Jews themselves have interacted with the Gentiles?

It is understandable that one might be Anti-Semitic if they were merely defending themselves from Jewish "Anti-Gentilism" prejudices. Doesn't this type of criticism go both ways? Is it fair that it is not politically correct to criticize the Zionist Government of Israel or for that matter an individual Jew? Why should any person or government entity be exempt from criticism?

Notable Quotes

"All the perplexities, confusions, and distresses in America arise, not from defects in the Constitution or confederation, not from want of honor or virtue, as much as from downright ignorance of the nature of coin, credit, and circulation."
John Adams

"There are two ways to conquer and enslave a nation. One is by the sword, the other is by debt."
John Adams

"The division of the United States into federations of equal force was decided long before the Civil War by the high financial powers of Europe. These bankers were afraid that the United States, if they remained as one block, and as one nation, would attain economic and financial independence, which would upset their financial domination over the world. The voice of the Rothschilds prevailed. Therefore, they sent their emissaries into the field to exploit the question of slavery to open an abyss between the two sections of the union."
Otto von Bismarck, Chancellor of Germany, 1876

"When a government is dependent upon bankers for money, they and not the leaders of the government control the situation, since the hand that gives is above the hand that takes…Money has no motherland; financiers are without patriotism and without decency;
their sole object is gain."
Napoleon Bonaparte, 1815

"It is advisable to do all in your power to sustain such prominent daily and weekly newspapers, especially the Agricultural and Religious Press, as well oppose the greenback issue of paper money and that you will also withhold patronage from all applicants who are not willing to oppose the government issue of money...To repeal the Act creating bank notes, or to restore to circulation the government issue of money will be to provide the people with money and will therefore seriously affect our individual profits as bankers and lenders. See your congressman at once and engage him to support our interests that we may control legislation."

Secretary James Buell, speaking at an American Bankers Association meeting, 1877

Edmund Burke (1729-1797) British Statesman and Philosopher. Burke's writings and speeches may be described as a defense of sound constitutional statesmanship against prevailing abuse and misgovernment. Burke was one of the foremost political thinkers of 18th century England.

The only thing necessary for evil to triumph is for good men to do nothing.
Edmund Burke

Senator Prescott Bush (1895-1972)
During his 1959 acceptance speech as the Alfalfa Club's presidential nominee, **Senator Prescott Bush** (President George Bush's grandfather) was reported as stating:
I recall here the immortal words of Granville Rice, when he wrote:

> *The rules of life apply the same*
> *To any sport you choose*
> *It matters not how you play the game,*
> *So long as you never lose.*

It looks like Senator Prescott Bush's son and grandson are carrying on the tradition of "It matters not how you play the game, So long as you never lose."

There are no such things as miracles; only natural laws which man has yet to understand.

Larry Flinchpaugh

Benjamin Franklin (1706-1790) He was born in Boston and was the tenth son of soap maker, Josiah Franklin. His mother was Abiah Folger, the second wife of Josiah. Young Benjamin loved to read and was an apprentice to his brother James, who was a printer. He helped to compose, set the type and then to distribute the pamphlets they printed.

In 1729, Benjamin Franklin bought a newspaper, the *Pennsylvania Gazette* and he often contributed articles to his own paper under aliases. His paper soon became very successful in the colonies and was one of the first papers to include political cartoons which were written by him.

In 1733 he began publishing *Poor Richard's Almanac*. It included such things as weather reports, recipes, predictions and homilies. Many of the famous phrases associated with Franklin, such as, "A penny saved is a penny earned" come from *Poor Richard's Almanac*.

In the 1720's and 1730's Franklin organized the "Junto" a group dedicated to self improvement and civic improvement. He also joined the Masons about this same period.

By 1749 he had retired from business and started concentrating on science, experiments, and inventions. He invented an efficient heating stove, called the Franklin Stove, swim fins, the glass armonica (a musical instrument) and bifocals.

He began to study electricity in the early 1750's. His observations, involving the nature of electricity and lightning brought Franklin international fame. He went to England and stayed until 1775, as a Colonial representative not only of Pennsylvania, but of Georgia, New Jersey and Massachusetts.

In 1765, he began to wonder if the American colonies should break free of England. Franklin was elected to the Second Continental Congress and worked on helping to draft the Declaration of Independence. Though much of the writing is Thomas Jefferson's, much of the contribution is Franklin's. In 1776 Franklin signed the Declaration of Independence, and afterward sailed to France as an ambassador to the Court of Louis XVI. The government of France not only signed a Treaty of Alliance with the Americans in 1778 but also secured loans for the Colonies. In his late seventies, Franklin became president of the Executive Council of Pennsylvania and served as a delegate to the Constitutional Convention whereby he signed the Constitution. One of his last public acts was writing an anti-slavery treatise in 1789.

Franklin died on April 17, 1790 at the age of 84. It is said that 20,000 people attended the funeral of the man who was called, "the harmonious human multitude."

Quotes by Benjamin Franklin

Light houses are more helpful than churches.

Half a truth is often a great lie.

The way to see by Faith is to shut the Eye of Reason.

To follow by faith alone is to follow blindly.

If men are so wicked with religion, what would they be if without it.

"You see, a legitimate government can both spend and lend money into circulation, while banks can only lend significant amounts of their promissory bank notes, for they can neither give away nor spend but a tiny fraction of the money the people need. Thus, when your bankers here in England place money in circulation, there is always a debt principal to be returned and usury to be paid. The result is that you have always too little credit in circulation to give the workers full employment. <u>You do not have too many workers, you have too little money in circulation</u>, and that which circulates, all bears the endless burden of unpayable debt and usury."

Benjamin Franklin, speaking at the London Parliament

"In the colonies, we issue our own money. It is called 'Colonial Scrip'. We issue it in proper proportion to the demands of trade and industry to make the goods pass easily from the producers to the consumers. In this manner, creating for ourselves our own paper money, we control its purchasing power and we have no interest to pay to anyone."

Benjamin Franklin, speaking at the London Parliament

"The refusal of George III to allow the colonies to operate an honest money system which freed the ordinary man from the clutches of the money manipulators was probably the Prime Cause of the Revolution."

 Benjamin Franklin

Barry Goldwater (1909-1998)   He was a five term United States Senator from Arizona. (1953-1965, 1969-1987) Barry Goldwater was the Republican Party's nominee for President in 1964 and was a Major General in the U.S. Air Force reserves

Quotes by Barry Goldwater

David Rockefeller's newest international cabal …it is intended to be the vehicle for multinational consolidation of the commercial and banking interests by seizing control of the political government of the United States.

Barry Goldwater -Writing about the Tri Lateral Commission

The income tax created more criminals than any other single act of government.

To disagree, one doesn't have to be disagreeable.

"Whomsoever controls the volume of money in any country is absolute master of all industry and commerce and when you realize that the entire system is very easily controlled, one way or another, by a few powerful men at the top, you will not have to be told how periods of inflation and depression originate."
James Garfield, assassinated within weeks of release of this statement during the first year of his presidency in 1881

"If all the bank loans were paid, no one could have a bank deposit, and there would not be a dollar of coin or currency in circulation. This is a staggering thought. We are completely dependent on the commercial banks. Someone has to borrow every dollar we have in circulation, cash or credit. If the banks create ample synthetic money we are prosperous; if not, we starve. We are absolutely without a permanent money system. When one gets a complete grasp of the picture, the tragic absurdity of our hopeless position is almost incredible, but there it is. It is the most important subject intelligent persons can investigate and reflect upon. It is so important that our present civilization may collapse unless it becomes widely understood and the defects remedied very soon."
Robert H. Hamphill, Credit Manager, Federal Reserve Bank of Atlanta

"The common enemy of humanity is man. In searching for a new enemy to unite us, we came up with the idea that pollution, the threat of global warming, water shortages, famine and the like would fit the bill. All these dangers are caused by human intervention, and it is only through changed attitudes and behavior that they can be overcome. The real enemy then, is humanity itself."

Richard Haass- Club of Rome

"World events do not occur by accident. They are made to happen, whether it is to do with national issues or commerce; most of them are staged and managed by those who hold the purse strings."
Denis Healey, former British Secretary of Defense

"Every Congressman, every Senator knows precisely what causes inflation...but can't, [won't] support the drastic reforms to stop it [repeal of the Federal Reserve Act] because it could cost him his job."
Robert A. Heinlein—Expanded Universe

"Very soon, every American will be required to register their biological property in a National system designed to keep track of the people and that will operate under the ancient system of pledging. By such methodology, we can compel people to submit to our agenda, which will affect our security as a chargeback for our fiat paper currency. Every American will be forced to register or suffer not being able to work and earn a living. They will be our chattel, and we will hold the security interest over them forever, by operation of the law merchant under the scheme of secured transactions. Americans, by unknowingly or unwittingly delivering the bills of lading to us will be rendered bankrupt and insolvent, forever to remain economic slaves through taxation, secured by their pledges. They will be stripped of their rights and given a commercial value designed to make us a profit and they will be none the wiser, for not one man in a million could ever figure our plans and, if by accident one or two would figure it out, we have in our arsenal plausible deniability. After all, this is the only logical way to fund government, by floating liens and debt to the registrants in the form of benefits and privileges. This will inevitably reap to us huge profits beyond our wildest expectations and leave every American a contributor to this fraud which we will call "Social Insurance." Without realizing it, every American will insure us for any loss we may incur and in this manner; every American will unknowingly be our servant, however begrudgingly. The people will become helpless and without any hope for their redemption and, we will employ the high office of the President of our dummy corporation to foment this plot against America."

Edward Mandell House, Presidential Foreign Policy Advisor, in a private meeting with President Wilson

---

"The real menace of our republic is this invisible government which like a giant octopus sprawls its slimy length over city, state and nation. It seizes in its long and powerful tentacles our executive officers, our legislative bodies, our schools, our courts, our newspapers, and every agency created for the public protection. Like the octopus of real life, it operates under cover of a self-created screen...At the head of this octopus are the Rockefeller Standard Oil interests and a small group of powerful banking houses generally referred to as *International Bankers*. The little coterie of powerful International Bankers *virtually run the United States government* for their own selfish purposes. They practically control both parties, write political platforms, make catspaws of party leaders, use the leading men of private organizations and resort to every device to place in nomination for high public office only such candidates as will be amenable to the dictates of corrupt big business. These International Bankers and Rockefeller Standard Oil interests control the majority of newspapers and magazines in this country."

John F. Hylan, New York City Mayor, New York Times, March 26, 1922

Quotes by Andrew Jackson

"You (International Bankers) are a *den of vipers and thieves*. I intend to rout you out, and by the Eternal God, I will rout you out. If the American people only understood the rank injustice of our money and banking system, there would be a revolution before morning."
Andrew Jackson, in an address to Congress, 1829

"The bold effort the present bank has made to control the Government, the distress it has wantonly produced...are but premonitions of the fate that awaits the American People should they be deluded into a perpetuation of this institution [The Bank of the United States], or the establishment of another like it."
Andrew Jackson

Thomas Jefferson (1743-1826) He was born April 13, 1743 in Shadwell, Virginia and later served in the Virginia House of Burgesses, Representing Virginia at the Continental Congress. He was educated at the William and Mary College and became a Lawyer.
Work History:

> 1767- Admitted to the Virginia bar.
> 1769- Elected to the Virginia House of burgesses
> 1775-76 Delegate to the Continental Congress
> 1776-79 Virginia House of Delegates
> 1779- Elected Governor of Virginia
> 1782-Dispatched to England to treat for peace with
> **Great Britain.**
> 1784-Associate Envoy to France

1785-Minister to the French Court
1789-Secretary of State
1793-Established the Democratic-Republican Party
1796-Vice President of the United States
1801-President of the United States
1803-More than doubled the size of the U.S.
      with the "Louisiana Purchase" from France
1810-Established the University of Virginia
1826- Died (July 4th)   Exactly 50 years after
    signing the Declaration of Independence.

Quotes by Thomas Jefferson

A democracy is nothing more than mob rule, where fifty-one percent of the people may take away the rights of the other forty-nine.

All tyranny needs to gain a foothold is for people of good conscience to remain silent.

Banking establishments are more dangerous than standing armies.

Commerce with all nations, alliance with none, should be our motto.

I do not find in orthodox Christianity one redeeming feature.
I find that the harder I work the more luck I seem to have.

I never considered a difference of opinion in politics, in religion, in philosophy, as cause for withdrawing from a friend.
In every country and every age, the priest had been hostile to liberty.

That government is best which governs the least, because its people discipline themselves.

The democracy will cease to exist when you take away from those who are willing to work and give to those who would not.

When the people fear their government, there is tyranny; when the government fears the people, there is liberty.

"The modern theory of the perpetuation of debt has drenched the earth with blood, and crushed its inhabitants under burdens ever accumulating."

I wish it were possible to obtain a single amendment to our Constitution - taking from the Federal Government their power of borrowing (from privately-owned corporate banks).

Quotes by Henry Kissinger

Control oil and you control nations; control food and you control the people.

The illegal we do immediately. The unconstitutional takes a little longer. New York Times, Oct. 28, 1973

Today Americans would be outraged if U.N. troops entered Los Angeles to restore order; tomorrow they will be grateful! This is especially true if they were told there was an outside threat from beyond **whether real or promulgated**, that threatened our very existence. It is then that all peoples of the world will pledge with world leaders to deliver them from this evil. The one thing every man fears is the unknown. When presented with this scenario, individual rights will be willingly relinquished for the guarantee of their well being granted to them by their world government."

Address to the Bilderbergers, May 21, 1992.

"But the whole scheme of a Federal Reserve Bank with its commercial-paper basis is an impractical, cumbersome machinery, is simply a cover, to find a way to secure the privilege of issuing money and to evade payment of as much tax upon circulation as possible, and then control the issue and maintain, instead of reduce, interest rates. It is a system that, if inaugurated, will prove to the advantage of the few and the detriment of the people of the United States. It will mean continued shortage of actual money and further extension of credits; for when there is a lack of real money people

have to borrow credit to their cost."

Alexander Lassen in a statement before the Senate Banking and Currency Committee, 1913

Abraham Lincoln (1809-1865) He was the sixteenth President of the United States who successfully led our country through its greatest crisis, the Civil War, and then was assassinated less than a month after the war's end.

Quotes by Abraham Lincoln

Study the constitution. Let it be preached from the pulpit, proclaimed in Legislatures, and enforced in Courts of Justices.

"I have two great enemies, the southern army in front of me and the financial institutions in the rear. Of the two, the one in the rear is the greatest enemy. *The Money Power preys upon the nation* in times of peace, and conspires against it in times of adversity. It is more despotic than monarchy, more insolent than autocracy, more selfish than bureaucracy. It denounces, as public enemies, all who question

its methods or throw light upon its crimes."

"*The Government should create, issue, and circulate all the currency and credits needed to satisfy the spending power of the Government and the buying power of consumers.* The privilege of creating and issuing money is not only the supreme prerogative of Government, but it is the Government's greatest creative opportunity. By the adoption of these principles…the taxpayers will be saved immense sums of interest [by **not** having to borrow

from **privately-owned** corporate banks]...Money will cease to be master and become the servant of humanity. Democracy will rise superior to the Money Power."
Abraham Lincoln, Senate Document 23, Page 91, 1865

"This (Federal Reserve) Act establishes the most gigantic trust [monopoly] on earth. When the President [Woodrow Wilson] signs this bill, *the invisible government* by the Monetary Power will be legalized. The people may not know it immediately, but the *day of reckoning is only a few years removed*. The trusts will soon realize that they have gone too far even for their own good. The people must make a declaration of independence to relieve themselves from the Monetary Power. This they will be able to do by taking control of Congress. Wall Streeters could not cheat us if you Senators and Representatives did not make a humbug of Congress...*The greatest crime of Congress is its currency system.* The worst legislative crime of the ages is perpetrated by this banking bill. The caucus and the party bosses have again operated and prevented the people from
getting the benefit of their own government."
Congressman Charles A. Lindbergh, Sr., 1913

"We (bankers) must proceed with caution and guard every move made, for the lower order of people are already showing signs of restless commotion. Prudence will therefore show a policy of apparently yielding to the popular will until our plans are so far consummated that we can declare our designs without fear of any organized resistance.

The Farmers Alliance and Knights of Labor organizations in the United States should be carefully watched by our trusted men, and we must take immediate steps to control these organizations in our interest or disrupt them. At the coming Omaha Convention to be held July 4th (1892), our men must attend and direct its movement, or else there will be set on foot such antagonism to our designs as may require force to overcome. This at the present time would be premature. We are not yet ready for such a crisis. Capital must protect itself in every possible manner through combination [conspiracy] and legislation. The courts must be called to our aid, debts must be collected, bonds and mortgages forclosed as rapidly as possible. When through the process of the law, the common people have lost their homes, they will be more tractable and easily governed through the influence of the strong arm of the government applied to a central power of imperial wealth under the control of the leading financiers. People without homes will not quarrel with their leaders.

History repeats itself in regular cycles. This truth is well known among our principal men who are engaged in forming an imperialism of the world. While they are doing this, the people must be kept in a state of political antagonism. The question of tariff reform must be urged through the organization known as the Democratic Party, and the question of protection with the reciprocity must be forced to view through the Republican Party. By thus *dividing voters*, we can get them to expend their energies in *fighting over questions of no importance* to us, except as teachers to the common herd. Thus, by discrete action, we can secure all that has been so generously planned and successfully accomplished."

Revealed by Congressman Charles A. Lindbergh before the U.S. Congress sometime during his term of office between the years of 1907 and 1917

"Banking doesn't involve fraud, banking is fraud."
Tim Madden-Monetary Historian

James Madison (1751-1836) He was brought up in Orange County Virginia and attended Princeton; then called the college of New Jersey. He participated in the framing of the Virginia Constitution in 1776, served in the Continental congress and was a leader in the Virginia assembly. Madison made a major contribution to the ratification of the Constitution by writing the Federalist essays with Alexander Hamilton and John Jay. Also, he helped frame the Bill of rights. He opposed Hamilton's financial proposals which he felt would unduly bestow wealth and power upon northern financiers. Out of this came the development of the Republican or Jeffersonian Party. Madison was elected President in 1808.

Quotes by James Madison

Each generation should be made to bear the burden of its own wars, instead of carrying them on, at the expense of other generations.

In no instance have... the churches been guardians of the liberties of the people.

The purpose of separation of church and state is to keep forever from these shores the ceaseless strife that has soaked the soil of Europe with blood for centuries.

It will be of little avail to the people that the laws are made by men of their own choice if the laws be so voluminous that they cannot be read or so incoherent that they cannot be understood.

"History records that the money changers have used every form of abuse, intrigue, deceit, and violent means possible to maintain their control over governments by controlling money and its issuance."

"I am afraid that ordinary citizens will not like to be told that the banks can, and do, create and destroy money. And they who control the credit of the nation direct the policy of governments, and hold in the hollow of their hands the destiny of the people."
Reginald McKenna, Chancellor of the Exchequer of England, 1924

If you think health care is expensive now, wait until you see what it costs when it's free.—**P. J. O'Rourke**

Thomas Paine (1737-1809) He was born in Thetford, England, and came to the United States at age 37, just in time to take part in the American Revolution. He had met Benjamin Franklin who had advised him to immigrate to the British Colonies in America and wrote him letters of recommendations. Paine left England in October and arrived in Philadelphia, Pennsylvania on November 30, 1774 after barely surviving the transatlantic voyage. He was an English pamphleteer, revolutionary, radical, classical liberal, inventor and intellectual. He was the author of the very popular pamphlet **"Common Sense"** which advocated independence for the American Colonies from Great Britain. Also he authored a series of pamphlets called **"The American Crisis"** from 1776-1783 that supported the American Revolution. In 1793-94 he wrote **"The Age of Reason"** which advocated "Deism" and took issue with Christian doctrines. The word "Deism" is the belief that there is a God that created the physical universe but does not interfere with it.

■■■

Paine was also an inventor and received a patent in Europe for a single span iron bridge, a smokeless candle and worked with John Fitch on the early development of steam engines.

Quotes by Thomas Paine

All national institutions of churches, whether Jewish, Christian or Turkish, appear to me no other than human inventions, set up to terrify and enslave mankind, and monopolize power and profit. Any system of religion that has anything in it that shocks the mind of a child cannot be true.

Belief in a cruel God makes a cruel man.

Is it not a species of blasphemy to call the New Testament revealed religion, when we see in it such contradictions and absurdities?

Of all the tyrannies that affect mankind, tyranny in religion is the worst.

One good schoolmaster is of more use than a hundred priests.

The Vatican is a dagger in the heart of Italy.

The whole religious complexion of the modern world is due to the absence from Jerusalem of a lunatic asylum.

There are matters in the Bible, said to be done by the express commandment of God, that are shocking to humanity and to every idea we have of moral justice.

The Christian religion is a parody on the worship of the Sun, in which they put a man whom they call Christ, in the place of the Sun, and pay him the same adoration which was originally paid to the Sun.

The bank hath benefit of interest on all moneys which it creates out of nothing."
Attributed to: ·William Peterson-(1658-1719) Founder of the Bank of England

---

"The powers of financial capitalism had (a) far-reaching aim, nothing less than to create a world system of financial control in private hands able to dominate the political system of each country and the economy of the world as a whole. This system was to be controlled in a feudalist fashion by the central banks of the world acting in concert, by secret agreements arrived at in frequent meetings and conferences. The apex of the systems was to be the Bank for International Settlements in Basel, Switzerland, a private bank owned and controlled by the world's central banks which were themselves private corporations. Each central bank...sought to dominate its government by its ability to control Treasury loans, to manipulate foreign exchanges, to influence the level of economic activity in the country, and to influence cooperative politicians by subsequent economic rewards in the business world."

Carroll Quigley

"I contend that we are both atheists. I just believe in one fewer god than you do. When you understand why you dismiss all the other possible gods, you will understand why I dismiss yours."
Stephen F. Roberts

"It [Central Bank] gives the National Bank almost complete control of national finance. Those few who understand the system [check book money and credit] will either be so interested in its profits, or so dependent on its favors, that there will be no opposition from that class, while on the other hand, the great body of the people, *mentally incapable of comprehending the tremendous advantage that capital derives from the system*, will bear its burden without complaint, and perhaps without even suspecting that the system is inimical [contrary] to their interests."
Rothschild Brothers of London, 1863

A government that robs Peter to pay Paul can always depend on the support of Paul.—**George Bernard Shaw**

"The modern banking system manufactures money out of nothing. The process is perhaps the most astounding piece of sleight of hand that was ever invented. *Banking was conceived in iniquity and was born in sin*. The Bankers own the earth. Take it away from them, but leave them the power to create money and control credit, and with the flick of the pen they will create enough

deposits to buy it all back again. However, take this great power away from them, and all the great fortunes like mine disappear, and they ought to disappear, for this would be a happier and better world to live in. But, *if you wish to remain the slaves of Bankers and pay the cost of your own slavery, let them continue to create money and control credit."*
Sir Josiah Stamp, Director of the Bank of England in the 1920s, reputed to be the second richest man in England at that time

..."If the Government schools are allowed to teach children K-12 using Pavlovian/Skinnerian animal training methods-which provide tangible rewards only for correct answers- there can be no freedom.   Why?   People "trained"-not educated- by such educational techniques will be fearful of taking principled, sometimes controversial, stands when called for because these people will have been programmed to speak up only if a positive reward or response is forthcoming".
Charlotte T. Iserbyt, "The Deliberate Dumbing Down of America"

The true equation is "democracy" = government by world financiers."
J.R.R. Tolkien, in "The Letters of J.R.R. Tolkien"

"Right after the Civil War there was considerable talk about reviving Lincoln's brief experiment with the Constitutional monetary system. Had not the European money-trust intervened, it would have no doubt become an established institution."
Dr. W. Cleon Skousen, author of *"The Naked Capitalist"* and *"The Naked Communist"*

"On Sept. 1st, 1894, we *will not* renew our loans under any consideration. On Sept. 1st we will demand our money. We will foreclose and become mortgagees in possession. *We can take two-thirds of the farms west of the Mississippi, and thousands of them east of the Mississippi as well, at our own price...*Then the farmers will become tenants as in England..."

<u>**Memo of the American Bankers Association, as printed in the US Congressional Record of April 29, 1891**</u>

"We have only one political party in the USA, the Democratic Republicans, and they just take turns lying to us."
<u>**[Unknown]**</u>

Hillary Clinton admits the Council on Foreign Relations controls Government Policy- August 2009

Hillary Clinton's remarks at the Council on Foreign Relations meeting, "...it's good to have an outpost of the Council right here down the street from the State Department. We get a lot of advice from the Council, so this will mean I won't have as far to go to be told what we should be doing." *Note: This unelected body should not be telling our Secretary of State what to do.*

Research Sources—Publications

Author's note: It is up to the researcher to determine the accuracy and validity of the suggested publications, documentaries, and web sites. These sources are very informative but should be verified by consulting more than one source.

American Free Press (Weekly newspaper)
(www.americanfreepress.com)
1-888-699-NEWS

The Barnes Review (Magazine)
645 Pennsylvania Avenue, SE
Suite 100
Washington Dc, 20003 (877-773-9077)
Republic Magazine
P O Box 10577
Newport Beach, California 92658
866-437-6570

Research Sources—Computer Web Sites

Air America (www.airamerica.com)

Alex Jones Prison Planet (www.prisonplanet.com) Also broadcasts on short wave radio.

American Jury Institute-www.americanjuryinstitute.org or www.fija.org

Conspiracy Reality TV Documentaries & Video (www.conspiracyrealitytv.com)

David Icke web site- www.davidicke.com

Deeper Truth Articles (www.deepertrutharticles.com)

Educate yourself www.Educate-yourself.org

Health www.healthfreedomusa.org

The Jeff Rense Program (www.rense.com)

Jordan Maxwell (www.jordanmaxwell.com

KFI 640 AM in Los Angeles California (www.kfi640am.com) "Coast to Coast AM"- hosted by George Noory. (Also carried on many other over the air radio stations)

The Library of Congress (**Search of House and Senate Bills**) (**www.thomas.loc.gov**

Ludwig von Mises Institute- www.mises.org

Republic Broadcasting Network (RBN- Daily radio programs on your computer) www.republicbroadcasting.org

Take Back Washington www.takebackwashington.com

You Tube (www.youtube.com)

We The People Radio net Work (www.wtprn.com)

What Really Happened (www.whatreallyhappened.com)

Research Sources—Movie Documentaries

America: Freedom to Fascism by Aaron Russo

In 2006 this movie debuted in theatres in select U.S. cities. This documentary covers many subjects. Including: the Internal Revenue Service (IRS), the income tax, Federal Reserve System, national ID cards, (Real ID Act), human-implanted RFID tags (Spy chips), Diebold electronic voting machines, globalization, Big Brother, taser weapon abuse and the alleged use of terrorism by government as a means to diminish the citizens' rights. (Run. Time 95 Minutes)

Zeitgeist, The Movie

This is a 2007 documentary film produced by Peter Joseph about Christianity, the attacks of 9/11, and the Federal Reserve Bank as well as a number of conspiracy theories related to those three main topics. It was released free on line via Google video in June of 2007

Zeitgeist won the top award for Best Feature Documentary/ Artivist Spirit at the 4th Annual Artivists awards in 2008 in Hollywood, Ca.

Zeitgeist Addendum

This second Zeitgeist documentary is a very thought provoking presentation but people like Alex Jones and G. Edward Griffin question some of the facts presented and its true agenda. Additional research can be found on the internet and a web site posted by "The Venus Project." (Google Video-over one hour long)

The Money Masters

The Money Masters is a fascinating documentary about the worldwide history of central banking and fractional reserve lending. It was made in 1998, but the information is still very relevant—even more so now than a decade ago. Despite being three and a half hours long and low-budget, it's an extremely gripping film. It opens by asking the following questions:

- What's going on in America today- why are we over our heads in debt?
- Why can't the politicians bring debt under control?
- Why are so many people working at low-paying, dead end jobs and still making do with less?
- What's the future of the American economy and way of life?

- Why does the government tell us that inflation is low when the buying power of our paychecks is declining at an alarming rate?
- Are we heading into an economic crash of unprecedented proportions? If so can we prevent it?
- What can we do to protect our families?

The entire film can be viewed on Google Video. (Running Time is 3 ½ hours)

9-11 Ripple Effect

96 minute documentary featuring Dave von Kleist- of "The Power Hour." Excellent presentation of the 9-11 attack questioning the government's explanation of events.

Cheney's Law

PBS production on "Nightline". This documentary describes how Vice President Dick Cheney conducted a secret behind closed doors campaign to give the President virtually unlimited wartime powers. This can be viewed free on the PBS web site.

Loose Change Final Cut -Loose Change Final Cut is the third installment of the documentary that asks the tough questions about the 9-11 attack and related events. The movie hopes to be a catalyst for a new independent investigation in which the family members receive answers to their questions and the true **PERPETRATORS** of this horrendous crime are **PROSECUTED** and **PUNISHED**. This documentary can be viewed for free on the internet.

Research Sources—Key Words

(Learn to "Google" key words that you find in this book and other books you read) **I.e. Anti-Semitic-Black Pope-Conspiracy Nuts-Economic Hit Man-Electoral College-False Flag Operation-Federal Reserve-Fractional Reserve Banking-Anti-Semitism Review Act of 2004-Holocaust Revisionists"-**

Inflation-Mossad-Mind Control-Presidential Directive 51-Propaganda-Republic form of government-Sixteenth Amendment-The Hegelian Dialectic-Thought Control-Trial by Jury-Teutonic Zionism-Warren Commission Report-Zionism

Research Sources—Suggested Reading

And the Truth Will Set You Free—by David Icke
The Age of Reason-- by Thomas Paine
*An Appeal To Reason-*The Writings of Willis A. Carto
Attention Deficit Democracy-- by James Bovard
The Biggest Secret—by David Icke
*Capitalism and Freedom--*by Milton Friedman
The Christ Conspiracy-The Greatest Story Ever Sold-- by Archarya S
Common Sense-- by Thomas Paine
Constitutional Chaos: What Happens When the Government Breaks Its Own Laws –by Andrew P. Napolitano
Corporatism-The Secret Government of the New World Order by Jeffrey Grupp
The David Icke Guide to Global Conspiracy (And How to End It.)
*The Day After Roswell—*by Philip J. Corso A former Pentagon official reveals the United States government's shocking UFO cover-up.
*The Deliberate Dumbing Down of America--*by Charlotte Thompson Iserbyt
The Draft: A Handbook of Facts and Alternatives-- by Sol Tax
The Economic Hit Man-- by John Perkins
The End of America-- by Naomi Wolf
The New Babylon—Those Who Reign Supreme "Inside the Rothschild Empire: The Modern Day Pharisees
*Freedom Under Siege--*by Ron Paul
How to Win Friends and Influence People and Five Essential People Skills: How to Assert Yourself, Listen to Others, and Resolve Conflict—by Dale Carnegie
*The Psychology of Winning—*by Denis Waitley

The Revolution- A Manifesto-- by Ron Paul

Rothschilds Money Trust—by George Armstrong (Buy at Amazon.com or free on the internet)

Seeds of Destructions-The Hidden Agenda of Genetic Manipulation-by F. William Engdahl

*The Terror Conspiracy—*by Jim Marrs

*Think and Grow Rich--*by Napoleon Hill

*The Tyranny of Good Intensions: How Prosecutors and Bureaucrats are Trampling the Constitution in the Name of Justice—*by Paul Craig Roberts and Lawrence M. Stratton.

Vietnam-Why Did We Go-The Religious Beginning of an Unholy War-- by Avro *Manhattan (1914-1990) the shocking story of the Catholic Church's role in starting the Vietnam War.*

War Made Easy: How Presidents and Pundits Keep Spinning Us to Death—by Norman Solomon.

*The Web of Debt—*by Ellen Hodgson Brown, J.D.

*What Has Government Done to Our Money?—*by Murray Rothbard

We Hold These Truths-The Hope of Monetary Reform—by Richard C. Cook

An excellent way to get involved as a "Political Activist" is to write "Letters to the Editor" of your local newspaper. Sharing your political views will help encourage others to do their own research and help them make better decisions in the voting booth.

The "Letters to the Editor" in your local paper is one of the most popular sections of any paper.

Flinchpaugh Gazette
Nov. 10, 2008

Abolish the "FED" Now

The recent bail outs approved by the leaders of both the Republican and Democrat parties should convince you that the Federal Reserve System must be abolished. Seeing what is happening on Wall Street, the real estate market, rising inflation and the financial problems of AIG, Bear Sterns, Lehman Brothers, etc should tell you that something is seriously wrong with our monetary system. When the <u>un</u>constitutional Federal Reserve Act was passed in 1913, it was supposed to protect the American economy from recessions, inflation and depressions. It obviously is not working very well. In fact, the dollar has lost 95% of its value due to inflation since the "Fed" began. The "Banksters" cause the so called "business cycles" to the detriment of us citizens but to the enormous benefit of these banking insiders. Under their control, they make billions of dollars whether in good economic times or {especially} in "bad times." Abolishing the "Fed" is the most important step we should take towards solving our financial problems.

In 1913 Congress unconstitutionally gave a private bank control of our country's monetary system by enacting the Federal Reserve Act. This gave the bankers the authority to create and print "Fiat" money with no backing and loan it to the United States government and *charge it interest*. Most people do not know that the Federal Reserve is not Federal and it has no reserves. In fact it is listed next to "Federal Express" in the business white pages of the phone book.

Also in 1913, the Sixteenth Amendment was passed authorizing an income tax to be collected based upon people's wages. Our country had operated fine for over 125 years with no income tax. Most of this individual income tax you pay to the IRS *does not* go to run the country. It mostly goes to pay the Federal Reserve for interest it charges for loaning us our own money! If anyone else does this, it is called counterfeiting and extortion.

Just think how much you personally could stimulate the economy and how much your living standard would increase if you were not required to pay income tax on your wages. Congress got us into this mess in 1913 and can get us out of it by repealing the Sixteenth Amendment and the Federal Reserve Act. An even easier way to abolish the "Fed" would be to have the president, by executive order, bypass the Federal Reserve and have the United States Treasury Department print *interest free* treasury notes. Since paper money doesn't last very long and needs to be replaced, in 2-3 years the Federal Reserve notes would no longer be in circulation and the unnecessary Federal Reserve would be out of business.

You hear very little from the politicians and the mainstream media about abolishing the Federal Reserve. The unconstitutionality and the massive thievery by the unnecessary "Fed" has been one of the biggest secrets ever kept from the American people. These central bankers are so rich and powerful they literally control the Democrat and Republican Party and the mainstream media.

Thomas Jefferson stated, "I believe that banking institutions are more dangerous to our liberties than standing armies. If the American people ever allow private banks to control the issue of their currency, first by inflation, then by deflation, the banks and corporations that will grow up around {the banks} will deprive the people of all property until their children wake up homeless on the continent their fathers conquered. The issuing power should be taken from the banks and restored to the people, to whom it properly belongs."

"It is well enough that the people of the nation do not understand our banking and monetary system, for if they did, I believe there would be a revolution before tomorrow morning."—**Henry Ford**

"Let me issue and control a nation's money and I care not who writes the laws."—**Mayer Rothschild**

"Most Americans have no real understanding of the operations of the international moneylenders...The accounts of the Federal Reserve have never been audited. It operates outside the **control**

of Congress and...manipulates the credit of the United States."—
Senator Barry Goldwater

It is your duty and obligation as an American citizen to get informed and pressure our representatives to do what is in the best interest of the masses of the people; not just the elite bankers.

Not a Shot Was Fired
Oct. 12, 2008

Presidential candidate, John McCain suggests that the Secretary of the Treasury buy up the troubled banks of this country. ---Good idea! While he is at it why not buy up General Motors, the oil companies, the airlines and maybe even Wal Mart. Then we can finally say that we have gone from a Democratic form of government to a Communist form of government without even a shot being fired.

America's Foreign Policy
Sept. 17, 2008

There are two opposing views on U.S. foreign policy, those of the "Nationalists" and those of the 'Internationalists" (Globalists). The Nationalist do not believe the people of the United States should meddle in the affairs of other countries and the Internationalist believes that the United States has an obligation to police the world and spread Democracy to all countries regardless the cost to the American taxpayer and the untold suffering our "elected" and "unelected" leaders cause in attempting to implement their inept and poorly conceived policies. I agree with what the "Nationalist" Thomas Jefferson said in 1801- **"I deem (one of) the essential principles of our government (to be) peace, commerce and honest friendship with all nations, entangling alliances with none..."**

The main objectives of U.S. foreign policy should be to simply protect our county from foreign invasion and engage in fair trade, but instead, it is being used to (1) protect America's supply of oil and oil company profits, (2) make money for the bankers and military industrial complex companies, and (3) fight Israel's wars. We, that is, major corporations and private importers, have the right to **buy** another country's oil but our nation **does not** have the right to invade a country and **take** their oil by economic-political intimidation or by brute force.

Throughout history, the "bankers" have been the source of so many of the world's problems. For example, if the bankers would refuse to finance the various countries that wanted war, wars would cease. Instead, history has proven that they finance both sides and have sometimes required the winning country to pay the debt of the losing country and then they make even more money in financing the reconstruction. Moreover, it seems that while military industrial complex companies make billions of dollars in profits from war, the common people (cannon fodder) give up their loved ones lives for an unjust cause, and their children and grandchildren are, for years, heavily taxed to pay for the war and inhumane foreign policies. Need I mention the hidden inflationary tax that we all pay immediately as the Federal Reserve prints more and more fiat money to finance these unjust wars? Remember the Federal Reserve, a private corporation, is not "'Federal" and they have no "Reserves".

One continually hears some of our government leaders and the public say, "Support our troops." I **do** support our troops, "Bring them home now!" They are **not** dying to protect our country; rather they are dying to protect the profits of Halliburton, Bechtel, Boeing, etc., and fighting Israel's war.

In the past I hesitated to infer that we are fighting **Israel's** war for fear of being falsely labeled anti-Semitic, which I am not. However after the United States passed the 2004 Anti-Semitic Act, it would appear that almost all Americans (including those of the Jewish faith) could be labeled as "Anti-Semitic". And, just because I don't support all the policies of the **Zionist** government of Israel, does not mean I dislike the majority of the Jewish people. Similarly, because I don't support President Bush's foreign policy of pre-emptive strikes does not make me anti-American.

I hear many people say, "We can't leave Iraq because the terrorists will follow us home." That just isn't true. When we left Vietnam, did we see the Viet Cong attacking Kansas City or New York? Having said this, however, I am extremely concerned about the Muslim terrorists and sleeper cells infiltrating our society, an issue which a more restrictive immigration policy and non intervention into the affairs of other nations could resolve. Our constant involvement in other countries' affairs is creating much resentment among their citizens. I wonder how the people and leaders of the United States would feel if China or Russia began to establish military bases with nuclear capability near our borders, say in Mexico, Canada or as Russia did in the 1960's, Cuba?

Unfortunately, neither Barack Obama nor John McCain will support the "Nationalists" foreign policy of non-intervention.

Voter Fraud
Jan. 17, 2008

Here we go again! We haven't even gotten to the presidential election and there are accusations of voter fraud in the Iowa caucus and the New Hampshire primary. I think there is still a large portion of Americans who believe that Al Gore should have been our president rather than George Bush. Why hasn't someone stepped up to be a leader and solve this problem? This is a sad commentary on our American system.

It has been proven to most of us that the electronic voting machines made by companies like "Diebold" are easily rigged but no one seems to know how to make them tamper proof. I admit that I don't have the knowledge to fix the computer problem but would like to suggest that all our votes have a consecutive "Reference number". After the election, the individual voter could go to his computer and verify that his reference number reflected his actual vote correctly.

It is extremely important to elect a president and congressional leaders that will reverse all of the unconstitutional programs initiated by George Bush and Dick Cheney; particularly the 'Patriot" Act.. We have gone from "the Department of War, to "The Department of Defense" to George Bush's "Department of Offense"

Joseph Stalin has been reported as saying, "Those who vote decide nothing. Those who count the votes decide everything".

We need to wake up America! Apathy is destroying our country. It's not too late to insist on our political leaders to make the necessary changes to regain our liberties as guaranteed by the constitution. However, we are rapidly approaching the time when the necessary changes will only be accomplished as the result of bloodshed as the United States approaches the third world status.

Fueling a Debate

Almost every day someone in the mass media attempts to explain why gasoline prices are so high. They continue to run stories showing our politicians calling for investigations into the oil companies' pricing practices and even propose charging the oil companies an excess profit tax. Some even say that OPEC controls the price.

There are two points that they all ignore! First there is no true energy shortage - just a shortage caused by our own government's inability to adopt the proper energy policy. Secondly, the oil companies' profits are not out of line when compared to other industries. You can't just say they make millions of dollars' profit. With millions invested they have to make millions. A better comparison can be made if you compare profit margins of the oil companies with other industries. When using this calculation, the profits of the oil companies are usually less than the pharmaceuticals and medicine, beverage, tobacco, and other industries.

Many geologists believe that the oil reserves and gas deposits in Alaska are as big as or bigger than those found in Saudi Arabia. The only problem is that we are not accessing this huge deposit of crude oil and gas. Naturally, with high demand and short supplies the price of gas will be high.

The 800-mile-long Alaskan pipeline from Prudhoe Bay to Valdez was completed in 1977 at a cost of more than $12 billion. The original estimate was $600 million, but due to our government's interference it cost billions of dollars more. Government regulations and bogus environmental concerns and red tape severely hampered its construction. It's almost like our government did not want the pipeline to be successful. The original pipeline was designed to pump 1.6 million barrels a day and an additional 48-foot pipe line was to be built next to it with a gas pipeline next to that. In addition to the huge reserve of crude oil, it was estimated that there was enough propane gas in Alaska to last us for the next 200 years.

In 1978 it pumped 1,087,695 bbls per day. By 1988, it was pumping 2,033,082 bbls per day. Since then it has gradually decreased to only 759,081 bbls per day in 2006. Someone in the government needs to explain why it is not pumping at its full capacity

There should be enough oil and gas in Alaska and other areas of the United States to make us completely energy independent in the next five years. In consideration of global warming and other environmental concerns, we should continue to develop alternative clean burning fuels like ethanol.

Once we become energy independent from the Middle Eastern countries we would have one less reason to interfere in other countries' affairs. Also, the price at the pump should come down as the supply matches the demand.

Wouldn't it be great to have gasoline drop to $1.50 a gallon? I think it could happen with the right energy policies.

Author's note: October 2008: Gas prices have dramatically been lowered, probably less from less demand than by Wall Street traders not trading crude oil through 15 to 20 trades.

FAUX (Fox) TV
Jan. 7, 2008

Have you ever questioned if the "FAUX" TV network was really "Fair and Balanced" as they claim? If you have paid close attention on how they are covering the presidential candidates', you may have some doubts.

Just recently they excluded republican Congressman Ron Paul and Representative Duncan Hunter from the New Hampshire debate. I guess they just wanted to include the top five candidates like Mike Huckabee, Mitt Romney, Rudy Giuliani, John McCain and Fred Thompson. Most of the Polls show that Ron Paul has a better chance of winning than Fred Thompson, yet he was excluded!

If you have ever watched "Hannity and Combs" and heard Sean talk about Ron Paul, it would be obvious that he is not being "Fair and Balanced" Sean was telling his viewers what a great job Fox News was doing in conducting one of their presidential candidate polls, but when Ron Paul won the poll, Sean made a comment that the poll in this case was inaccurate because all the internet fans of Ron Paul had skewed the results by massive call ins. I guess no other candidate's support groups would have stooped so low as to support their candidate in this manner. One of Ron Paul's supporters admitted that he tried to call in twice but got a recording that only one vote per telephone number would be accepted. I guess Sean didn't know this about his own poll procedures.

Also when you continually hear Fox TV personalities like Sean and guests like neoconservative Bill Kristol from the "Weekly Standard" refer to Congressman Ron Paul as a fringe candidate with no chance of winning, you begin to wonder just what is the agenda of FOX News. Do a Google search of Bill Kristol and his father, Irving Kristol if you would like to get a better in depth view of Fox Networks true views. To get a better in depth view of Congressman Ron Paul's views, do a Google search on "You Tube" or go to www.ronpaul2008.com. You will find that Ron Paul represents the 70% of us who are dissatisfied with our president and congress.

As Sheppard Smith of FOX News says 'We Report, You Decide" I have decided, FOX News is definitely not "Fair and balanced"

Road Map for Peace
Sept. 6, 2007

Most of us think that the Middle East conflict is just between Israel and the Palestinians. There is the Zionist Jewish government, the Israeli Mossad (Similar to America's CIA), Jews living in Israel and in other parts of the world and the PLO, Hamas, Fatah, etc., all of which have many different viewpoints and agendas. The United States is involved in providing money, arms and training, resulting in huge profits for the weapons manufacturers and financiers, but causing the entire world to suffer from the loss of lives, higher taxes and deplorable living conditions for millions of people.

It's unbelievable to me that the focus of the conflict seems to be based on such a small territory. The land mass of Israel would fit into the United States 768 times. In 1923, when the British divided the "Palestine" portion of the Ottoman Empire into two separate areas, Jewish Palestinians got that portion west of the Jordan River (25 percent) and the Arab Palestinians got that portion east of the Jordan River (75 percent) for an Arab Palestinian state. The Arab Palestinians do have a "homeland." It is called "Jordan."

It is horrible to see how fanatical religious differences play in this conflict. I don't believe the Jews are God's chosen people anymore than anyone else who follow the commandments of Moses. The Bible, Talmud and Koran appear to be about 75 percent mythology and 25 percent fact. My idea of a religion is a belief in a Creator, the Golden Rule and the love of your fellow man. Pretty simple.

The present Palestinian refugee camps need to be abandoned and the Arab countries in the world should accept these refugees into their own countries. For Israel's own security, the West Bank and the Gaza strip must remain a part of Israel.(*) Any Arab Palestinian who was forced to leave property they owned should be compensated.

Even if you agree with the United Nations resolutions making the Gaza Strip and West Bank a Palestinian state, why not just accept the fact that they lost the war in 1967 and should get on with their lives. It seems the Palestinians are more interested in killing Jews and denying Israel's right to exist than in establishing a homeland in an area they never had to begin with. The United States needs to stop the Israeli lobby from dictating America's foreign policy. America's foreign policy continues to create more terrorists. An American attack on Iran will create even more. We need to elect a leader like Congressman Ron Paul, Republican presidential candidate, or a Democrat who will not be unduly influenced by the lobbying groups. Our president, no matter which party they belong to, must promote foreign policies that will end the hostilities in the Middle East.

(*)Author's note, February 2009: I now believe, Israel must remove its settlements in the Gaza strip and West bank allowing the Palestinians access to their own land. Israel must halt all their settlements (Colonization) if there is ever to be peace in the Middle East.

News Sources
Jan. 8, 2007

With a hundred or more cable TV channels available, there is no legitimate reason why the American public cannot receive news programs from other countries like France, Italy, etc. This would give us a different perspective from the current news sources.

A quick look at the world wide news coming from other countries and even the Aljazeera web site, will open your eyes to the fact that there are many countries and news organizations that have different views on news pertaining to the U.S. It seems like the American people should have easier access to this information rather than searching the internet.

In the 1950's, when I was growing up in St. Joe, I remember my excitement buying a shortwave radio from Acme Radio that received an English language news program from Russia. It was interesting to note the differences in each countries views and trying to determine which one was telling the truth. At the time I was sure that the American news broadcast was most accurate and truthful.

As a college student I had to write a term paper that would be a large part of my grade. I needed a subject that would be so clever and interesting that even if it were not written very well, I would at least get a high mark for the idea. I decided to write several different news papers in different parts of the United States and request that they all send me a copy of their paper on the same day. I wanted to compare their news stories and determine if they reported the news fairly.

Fortunately, I had chosen the day Martin Luther King was arrested in a demonstration in the South. The southern newspaper had Kings Story on the front page with a large picture of him being thrown into a police "Paddy Wagon". The head lines of the story were huge. **"King Arrested in Demonstration"**. The De Moines, Iowa paper had the same story on page six with a postage stamp size picture of Mr. King dressed in a suit and tie and the head line was **"King Detained"**. The East and West coast papers had varying degrees of differences somewhere in between the paper in the South and the paper in Iowa.

It was interesting to see how the same news story could be portrayed differently because of its geographic location and the attitude of the editors and readers.

It is important for us to have multiple sources of information so we can get closer to the truth and make it difficult for those in power to purposely lie to us.

American To Do List
June 6, 2007

I would like to express some of my ideas on things that I strongly feel need to be done by our great country to keep it great and to encourage your readers to demand more from our politicians to make it happen.

1 Iraq- It seems that the majority of the people in this country believe that it is time for us to retreat from Iraq or should I say "Re-Deploy",. As they say there are no good choices, just better bad choices. We cannot continue to fight a war on Terrorism using conventional means like we did in Viet Nam. Has any one noticed Viet Nam is better off now that we left. I haven't heard of any Viet Cong being found in New York or Kansas City.

I would like to hear someone seriously discuss the idea of dividing Iraq into three states; Shiite, Sunni and Kurds. Why not give each Iraq adult citizen a monetary stake as well as a political stake in their country. The Iraq government could set up a Government owned Oil Company that would divide the profits; 1/3 to rebuild the country, 1/3 for investment and 1/3 to be paid twice a year to each Iraq citizen. I believe that Alaska and Saudi Arabia do this now. The American military should only protect the oil refineries and distribution facilities and let the Iraq government police their own country. Start building entire new towns that could be controlled and leave rebuilding cities like Baghdad until after the hostilities stop.

Since we have been assured by our Government that we did not go into Iraq for oil, I'm sure that the government and American oil companies would not object to this idea or at least something similar.

2 Eliminate or greatly reduce the power lobby groups have over our congress. Especially the control Israel has on our legislature.

No country except America should be in charge of our foreign policy. If Israel wants this much control over our foreign policy we should make them the 51st state. "No, I am not anti-Semitic"! I have nothing against the Jewish people, just the Zionist Jews running the country. When most people in other countries say they hate Americans, most are really saying they like the American people but hate the United States government's policies. Anyone should be able to criticize Israel and have it be understood that they are against Israel's government policies and not individual Jews.

3 Congress should abolish the Federal Reserve System which by the way is not "Federal" and they have no "Reserves". In 1776 our constitution gave the power to print money to the congress of the United States; not to a private company. In 1913 congress was some how convinced to set up the Federal Reserve to control our nation's money supply. When the government needs money it has to borrow it from the Federal Reserve and pay them interest. The United States tax payers have to pay a high rate of income tax just to pay this interest. I don't think it was a coincident that also in 1913 the Federal Income tax went into effect! If the Federal Reserve was abolished we might not even need a Federal income tax! (at least after the federal budget was balanced)

President Kennedy printed a large amount of US Treasury notes bypassing the Federal Reserve and the Interest. After Kennedy died these notes were recalled and taken out of circulation. I wonder if there is any connection between this action and his assassination.

I am tired of hearing arguments on whether gays should be allowed to get married. Of course they shouldn't! The definition of marriage is a union between a man and a woman. Why not just call it a "Same Sex Union" and give them the same rights as a married couple.

Let's elect leaders in the 2008 election that will address these issues and those that are in the best interest of the entire American population and not just the power elite!

Nevada Presidential Primary
Jan. 24, 2008

Once again the news media has marginalized Congressman Ron Paul while covering the Nevada primary. Saturday, I watched ABC, CBS, NBC, CNN and Fox News to see if they would report him fairly. They stayed true to form and almost completely ignored him even though he won 14% of the votes beating McCain, Huckabee, Thompson, Giuliani and Hunter.

Wolf Blitzer barely mentioned Ron Paul's surge in the Nevada poll and then spent about four minutes airing a piece about John Edwards and then personally interviewing Rudy Giuliani live for almost 5 minutes even though Rudy had only received 4% of the republican votes. Edwards had only 4% of the democrat vote.

The other networks also failed to mention anything about Ron Paul's success. To make things even worse, Dick Morris, a frequent guest of Fox News, called Thompson a name that I had never heard of before and referred to Ron Paul as a "Flake". It should be obvious to anyone closely watching the news being reported that the main stream media, or more specifically the people controlling the main stream media, definitely don't want Ron Paul to become president. Hopefully for Ron Paul's campaign, the public will react to this sinister display of censorship and will vote in huge numbers in favor of Ron Paul to demonstrate that they will not let these special interest groups dictate who they should vote for president.

Gandhi once said that "First they ignore you, then they ridicule you, then they fight you, then you win". Ron Paul and his ideology is in the final stages of winning. Probably the worst fear the elites have is that more and more people are beginning to understand that it just might be possible to eliminate the IRS and the Federal Reserve System. Just think if the people of St. Joe did not have to pay income tax on their salaries. The additional spending into our local economy would be much more beneficial than sending it to the Federal Reserve System. Most people would say, "How would our government operate without this tax money"? It would be easy because the taxes collected on your salary aren't being used for services. It pays the Federal Reserve for interest they charge our government for the fiat money they print out of thin air! The remaining corporate income tax that is legal according to our constitution, plus gasoline taxes, tariffs, etc. would be more than enough to pay the government's expenses; especially if we were to reduce our military bases spread throughout the world.

The United States currently has 702 overseas bases in about 130 countries. By eliminating many of these bases, enough money could be saved in this area alone to not only get us out of debt but also pay back all the money that has been borrowed from the Social security fund.

Ron Paul's ideas are not as crazy as many people think. As time goes on more and more of the electorate and our federal and state representatives are beginning to understand his message. The people who should be worried are the Federal Reserve Bankers and the world banking cartels. The rest of us will see a dramatic improvement in the quality of life when the IRS and the Federal Reserve are abolished. If the mass news media would start reporting congressman Ron Paul's views as much as the other candidates, the people of this country would finally understand what needs to be done to return our country to being one based on constitutional law instead of presidential decrees.

Criticism by Local Political Activist
June 27, 2007

This letter is in response to your criticism of my "Letter to the Editor" that appeared in the "Saint Joseph Telegraph" a couple of weeks ago. I felt that your comments were somewhat arrogant, misinformed and un-professional, especially considering your position in the XXXXXXX. I would have thought you would have been a little more tactful and respectful of another person's opinion but perhaps you were only doing what most politicians do best, that is, make an attempt to discredit his opponent rather than offering any real and meaningful solution. I feel very uncomfortable in addressing your criticism of my letter, but feel that I have little choice when you choose to show me such little respect.

Probably the most irritating to me was your comments alluding to the fact that I was "Anti-Semitic" and a "Conspiracy Theorist". Then you emphasized the fact that you were Jewish and referred to my "policy gurus". I am not sure who my "policy gurus" are or what you mean by that but it certainly doesn't sound complimentary.

Maybe I should give you my definition of "Anti-Semitic": A person who believes that Israel should be wiped off the face of the earth, the belief that the Holocaust never happened, and that all Jews should be killed. This is definitely not my belief and I resent anyone assuming that this is my belief simply because I criticize Israel's governmental policies. Can't anyone criticize the Israeli government's policies without being labeled "Anti-Semitic" by the ADL, the mass media or in this case the XXXXXX of the XXX. I criticize President Bush's policy almost daily and don't consider myself as being "Anti American". In a democracy it is our duty to offer   criticism to our government officials so they can properly represent their electors. It is very upsetting to me to see the ADL and people like you exploiting "Anti-Semitism and conspiracy theorist in order to silence your opponents. This makes me even more suspicious of your true agenda.

Since you made a point of informing me that you are Jewish, let me explain briefly my religious beliefs. I grew up attending the Westminster Presbyterian Church at 21st and Jules street here in St. Joseph in the 40s and 50s. As I got older, I found myself questioning the Christian religion and started studying the religions of the world. I just couldn't accept a lot of the religious doctrine presented by the churches. Also I had a great deal of difficulty understanding the church's treatment of the Indians in the 1800s and the Blacks in the 1900s. Why didn't the millions of good Christians and Jews solve these problems? A few years ago "I finally abandoned organized religion and discovered spirituality." I believe in a creator or higher intelligence, call it God if you wish, in the Golden Rule, the love and respect of your fellow man, and that one should attempt to improve the lives of everyone he meets. This is a fairly simple concept that frees one from making irrational decisions based on the mythology of any holy book like the Christian Bible, Talmud or Koran. My God does not have a chosen people or make any promises regarding the establishment of countries' boundaries.

The entire world is now suffering due to the establishment of the state of Israel in 1948. I think it was a huge mistake to have given Israel land that had belonged to the Palestinians. In fact there are large numbers of Jewish people that also believe this. I understand that this was partly justified by the Holocaust. The Holocaust was a terrible event in the worlds' history, but to keep it in perspective, it has been reported that Stalin killed an equal number of Russian citizens, the Chinese lost several million in WWII and the Allied troops lost millions. The Jewish people are not the only ones who suffered during that period.

I would think that the Palestinians would accept the fact that they lost the war and would move on with their lives. However if my land and property were confiscated to make room for Israel and I was forced to live in refugee camps, I might even consider becoming a suicide bomber. The Palestinians are desperate. The Israeli government should abide by the United Nations resolution and vacate the Gaza Strip and the West Bank so the Palestinians can re-establish themselves in the land they were forced to vacate.

The fact that the United States needs oil does not justify us meddling in the affairs of other countries. The only right we have is to buy their oil if they wish to sell it to us. There is plenty of energy resources in this country to sustain us for the next 100 years. The so called energy crisis keeps the gasoline prices high, helps the oil company's bottom line and gives us an excuse to wage war around the world. War is big business for the corporations and very profitable for them and the international banks but is devastating to the masses of the people in terms of war casualties and high taxes. I was a manager for "The Oil and Shale Corporation" for several years before retiring. (TOSCO)

In your opening statement you say, "If you want to be taken seriously, you need to step back from using conspiracy "Theorists" as your primary source of issues." I definitely do not use "conspiracy theorists" as my primary source of information. I do believe that conspiracy theorists have exposed a lot of issues that need to be further explained. Some of their theories have been explained but some do raise some important questions. If even 10 % proved to have some validity, they should be fully investigated. I think you are extremely naïve to believe that this country's leaders never engage in clandestine operations of very questionable legal and ethical matters. Just look at what is being done out in the open in regard to the passage of the 'Patriot Act".

You made a comment about my views as being off the pages of anti-government. I simply want our president to uphold the constitution and want our representatives to represent the best interest of the people who elected them and not the lobbyists who control them through donations of large sums of money or various other questionable perks.

Should I be ashamed about having Libertarian views on our drug policies? I think you are showing your lack of understanding of alternative viewpoints. I don't consider myself a 100% Libertarian, Conservative or Liberal. It depends on the issue being discussed.

About the CRS you are absolutely correct. The CRS does still exist. I didn't say they were abolishing all their services. It is my understanding that they are to stop preparing reports to congress analyzing Bills before congress. I think they should continue analyzing bills and even reporting to the public the originator and supporters of the "Pork Provisions".

My letter was intended to encourage discussion of some important issues that I feel get little attention in the main stream press. I appreciate your taking the time to respond to my letter but only wished you had been more respectful of my views. I am sure that there are some flaws in some of my views but overall there are some good points to consider. I have spent the last 50 years developing my views on religion and politics.

I would like to suggest that you go to"You Tube" and view the many videos featuring Ron Paul. Also look at his web page and maybe then you won't be so frightened of a Republican who has many Libertarian views.

Just Set the Furniture on Fire
Aug. 30, 2008

Last week, C-Span aired the National Institute of Science and Technology explanation of how World Trade Center Building Seven collapsed on 9/11. Building Seven collapsed even though no plane had hit it. The government's explanation was that the heat from the office furniture fires was so great the long span of the steel beams were weakened and caused the 47 story building to collapse in almost free-fall speed of 6 ½ seconds.

Hopefully, some of the demolition companies were watching this enlightening broadcast. The next time they need to demolish a large building, they might want to consider simply lighting the office furniture, rather than spending thousands of dollars installing the hundreds of small charges previously needed to bring down a skyscraper.

Authors Note: Of course this was meant to be a sarcastic comment on a government agencies ridiculous explanation on how the World Trade Center Seven building collapsed. I learned that not all people will recognize sarcasm. Following is a remark to my article by another reader of the newspaper who didn't recognize my sarcasm:

"In a response to a recent letter to the editor I can think of at least three reasons why you wouldn't take a sky scraper down by lighting the office furniture on fire. The first would easily be safety, by placing small charges throughout the building you have complete control over how, when and where the building falls, unlike with an office furniture fire. Number two, obviously, would be expense. I don't know how much those charges they use to tear down skyscrapers cost, but compared to the expense of people in a skyscraper lighting all the office furniture on fire, I'm sure the fire is more expensive. Number three, that If you are taking a skyscraper down for demolishment, you know, I doubt if there's any office furniture left in it anyway."

This reader's comment on my letter illustrates how easily the government and the controlled mainstream media can manipulate the public's opinion. I wrongly assumed that it would be obvious to anyone reading my letter that the building **did not collapse** due to the office furniture burning.

Averting a Financial Collapse
November 27, 2008

Many of those that read my earlier letter requesting the American voter to support the politicians that would abolish the Federal Reserve and income taxes on our salaries may think that this is an insane idea. I have had friends of mine say, "How would we pay for our schools, highways, and other government services?" What they don't realize is that the income tax collected on our wages goes mainly to pay for the interest the unnecessary, private Federal Reserve charges our government for loaning us **our own money**. Local county property taxes pays for our schools and the federal and state motor fuel tax pays for our highway system.

Ever since the Federal Reserve Act and the 16th Amendment authorizing tax on our salaries was passed in 1913, the entire world has had to suffer from this unconstitutional and evil act. The average person is not aware of the part played by our banking system in getting the United States involved in World War 1 and World War ll. The international bankers, which include our Federal Reserve, supported a war against Germany and Japan. Germany in 1939 and Japan in 1942 had bypassed their private banks and adopted a money system where the **state** created the money supply at **zero interest**. The international bankers were afraid that other countries would replicate this superior banking system. This was a serious threat to the private investors of the

United States Federal Reserve and a world war would be one way of countering it. Of course this is not the only cause of World War ll, but the banking issue isn't even discussed as a cause for the war.

Just think how much you personally could stimulate the economy and how much your living standard would improve if you were not required to pay income tax on your salary. In fact, this tax is a form of slavery.

Henry Ford said, "It is well enough that the people of the nation do not understand our banking and monetary system, for if they did, I believe there would be a revolution before tomorrow morning."

Senator Barry Goldwater "Most Americans have no real understanding of the operations of the international moneylenders...The accounts of the Federal Reserve have never been audited. It operates outside the control of Congress and...manipulates the credit of the United States."

It is very disheartening to see that none of our elected politicians (except Ron Paul) or news media celebrities even discuss this issue. The American people have not been given the facts about our current monetary system. Maybe if more people would seriously investigate the Federal Reserve's shortcomings, we could make the necessary changes to save our country from a financial collapse.

Economic Stimulus Bailout
February 20, 2009

A couple of weeks ago, a TV news reporter asked his guest if they believed the "Economic Stimulus" plan was going to work. The guest said, "Absolutely." "It will increase the debt and will increase the size of our government." I thought, "Wow, this guy hit the nail on the head." Not expecting such an honest answer the reporter immediately switched to another subject. Why won't the controlled mainstream media or our elected representatives discuss what really needs to be done to fix our economic problems?

Just a few months ago we were arguing the merits of passing a bailout stimulus package. At that time the only ones who approved of the bailouts were the Investment Bankers and their congressional cronies, Nancy Pelosi, Harry Reid and both presidential candidates. It didn't seem to matter that millions of American citizens' did not support the bailout.

Why would anyone in their right mind support bailing out those companies that made very poor management decisions with some even engaged in criminal activity plus paying their executives enormous salaries and bonuses as they were going broke. Bailing out these companies is no different than bailing out Las Vegas gamblers.

Today the propaganda machine has convinced most of the "sheeple" that it was necessary and the right thing to do. Many people seem to believe that it is the federal government's responsibility to solve all of our problems by redistributing the wealth. This kind of reasoning will eventually cause our whole system to collapse. We will never get out of debt and solve our economic problems until the Federal Reserve and fractional banking are abolished.

The bailout stimulus package is doing the same thing that got us into this mess in the first place; devaluating our existing dollars by printing more and more fiat money to finance the bailout.

Our present deplorable economic status is probably normal considering our governments failed monetary policies. What we thought was normal earlier was based on our governments polices of unlimited credit for everyone.

Why the Original Constitution Will Never Be Obsolete

(Reference "The 5000 Year Leap" by W. Cleon Skousen)

...Anyone who says the American Constitution is obsolete just because social and economic conditions have changed does not understand the real genius of the Constitution. It was designed to control something which **has not changed and will not change—namely, human nature.**

First Continental Congress (1774)

The First Continental Congress was a convention of delegates from twelve British North American Colonies. It was called in response to the passage of the Intolerable Acts by the British Parliament. It was held in Philadelphia and attended by 55 members from the legislatures of the 13 Colonies. The Province of Georgia did not send any delegates.

They met to discuss options, organize an economic boycott of British trade, publish a list of rights and grievances and petition king George for redress of those grievances.

They also called for another Continental Congress in the event that their petition was unsuccessful. Their appeal to the Crown had no effect so the second Continental Congress was convened the following year.

Second Continental Congress (July 4th 1776)
Adopted Declaration of Independence (5) parts and the Articles of Confederation

- **(1) Introduction**
- **(2) Preamble**
- **(3) Indictment of George lll**
- **(4) Denunciation of the British People**
- **(5) Conclusion**

The Second Continental Congress was a delegation of sixty five representatives from the legislatures of the thirteen British North American colonies that met from May 10, 1775 to March 1, 1781.

They adopted the Declaration of Independence and the articles of Confederation. It acted as the de facto U.S. national government by raising armies, directing strategy, appointing diplomats, and making formal treaties.

Articles of Confederation

The Articles of Confederation was the first governing constitution of the United States of America. The final draft was adopted by the Second Continental Congress on November 15, 1777 in York, Pennsylvania. It was finally ratified on March 1, 1781. The Confederation was capable of making war, negotiating diplomatic agreements, and resolving issues regarding the western territories. It could mint coins and borrow inside and outside the United States. The Articles were replaced by the United States Constitution on June 21, 1788.

United States Constitution

Preamble

We the People of the United States, in Order to form a more perfect Union, establish Justice, insure <u>domestic Tranquility,</u> provide for the common <u>defense</u>, promote the general <u>Welfare</u>, and secure the Blessings of Liberty to ourselves and our <u>Posterity,</u> do <u>ordain</u> and establish this Constitution for the United States of America.

Article I-- Legislative Branch

Section 1 - The Legislature-- All legislative Powers herein granted shall be vested in a Congress of the United States, which shall consist of a Senate and House of Representatives.

Section 2 - The House--The House of Representatives shall be composed of Members chosen every second Year by the People of the several States, and the Electors in each State shall have the Qualifications requisite for Electors of the most numerous Branch of the State Legislature.

No Person shall be a Representative who shall not have attained to the Age of twenty five Years, and been seven Years a Citizen of the United States, and who shall not, when elected, be an Inhabitant of that State in which he shall be chosen.

(Representatives and direct Taxes shall be apportioned *among the several States which may be included within this Union, according to their respective Numbers, which shall be determined by adding to the whole Number of free Persons, including those bound to Service for a Term of Years, and excluding Indians not taxed, three fifths of all other Persons.)* **(The previous sentence in parentheses was modified by the 14th Amendment, section 2.)** The actual Enumeration shall be made within three Years after the first Meeting of the Congress of the United States, and within every subsequent Term of ten Years, in such Manner as they shall by Law direct. The Number of Representatives shall not exceed one for every thirty Thousand, but each State shall have at Least one Representative; and until such enumeration shall be made, the State of New Hampshire shall be entitled to chuse three, Massachusetts eight, Rhode Island and Providence Plantations one, Connecticut five, New York six, New Jersey four, Pennsylvania eight, Delaware one, Maryland six, Virginia ten, North Carolina five, South Carolina five and Georgia three.

When vacancies happen in the Representation from any State, the Executive Authority thereof shall issue Writs of Election to fill such Vacancies.

The House of Representatives shall chuse their Speaker and other Officers; and shall have the sole Power of Impeachment.

Section 3 - The Senate--The Senate of the United States shall be composed of two Senators from each State, *(chosen by the Legislature thereof,)* **(The preceding words in parentheses superseded by 17th Amendment, section 1.)** for six Years; and each Senator shall have one Vote.

Immediately after they shall be assembled in Consequence of the first Election, they shall be divided as equally as may be into three Classes. The Seats of the Senators of the first Class shall be vacated at the Expiration of the second Year, of the second Class at the Expiration of the fourth Year, and of the third Class at the Expiration of the sixth Year, so that one third may be chosen every second Year; *(and if Vacancies happen by Resignation, or otherwise, during the Recess of the Legislature of any State, the Executive thereof may make temporary Appointments until the next Meeting of the Legislature, which shall then fill such Vacancies.)* **(The preceding words in parentheses were superseded by the 17th Amendment, section 2.)**

No person shall be a Senator who shall not have attained to the Age of thirty Years, and been nine Years a Citizen of the United States, and who shall not, when elected, be an Inhabitant of that State for which he shall be chosen.

The Vice President of the United States shall be President of the Senate, but shall have no Vote, unless they be equally divided.

The Senate shall choose their other Officers, and also a President pro tempore, in the absence of the Vice President, or when he shall exercise the Office of President of the United States.

The Senate shall have the sole Power to try all Impeachments. When sitting for that Purpose, they shall be on Oath or Affirmation. When the President of the United States is tried, the Chief Justice shall preside: And no Person shall be convicted without the Concurrence of two thirds of the Members present.

Judgment in Cases of Impeachment shall not extend further than to removal from Office, and disqualification to hold and enjoy any Office of honor, Trust or Profit under the United States: but the Party convicted shall nevertheless be liable and subject to Indictment, Trial, Judgment and Punishment, according to Law.

Section 4 - Elections, Meetings--The Times, Places and Manner of holding Elections for Senators and Representatives, shall be prescribed in each State by the Legislature thereof; but the Congress may at any time by Law make or alter such Regulations, except as to the Place of Choosing Senators.

The Congress shall assemble at least once in every Year, and such Meeting shall *(be on the first Monday in December,)* **(The preceding**

words in parentheses were superseded by the 20th Amendment, section 2.) unless they shall by Law appoint a different Day.

Section 5 - Membership, Rules, Journals, Adjournment--Each House shall be the Judge of the Elections, Returns and Qualifications of its own Members, and a Majority of each shall constitute a Quorum to do Business; but a smaller number may adjourn from day to day, and may be authorized to compel the Attendance of absent Members, in such Manner, and under such Penalties as each House may provide.

Each House may determine the Rules of its Proceedings, punish its Members for disorderly Behavior, and, with the Concurrence of two-thirds, expel a Member.

Each House shall keep a Journal of its Proceedings, and from time to time publish the same, excepting such Parts as may in their Judgment require Secrecy; and the Yeas and Nays of the Members of either House on any question shall, at the Desire of one fifth of those Present, be entered on the Journal.

Neither House, during the Session of Congress, shall, without the Consent of the other, adjourn for more than three days, nor to any other Place than that in which the two Houses shall be sitting.

Section 6 – Compensation--*(The Senators and Representatives shall receive a Compensation for their Services, to be ascertained by Law, and paid out of the Treasury of the United States.)* **(The preceding words in parentheses were modified by the 27th Amendment.)** They shall in all Cases, except Treason, Felony and Breach of the Peace, be privileged from Arrest during their Attendance at the Session of their respective Houses, and in going to and returning from the same; and for any Speech or Debate in either House, they shall not be questioned in any other Place.

No Senator or Representative shall, during the Time for which he was elected, be appointed to any civil Office under the Authority of the United States which shall have been created, or the Emoluments whereof shall have been increased during such time; and no Person holding any Office under the United States, shall be a Member of either House during his Continuance in Office.

Section 7 - Revenue Bills, Legislative Process, Presidential Veto--All bills for raising Revenue shall originate in the House of Representatives; but the Senate may propose or concur with Amendments as on other Bills.

Every Bill which shall have passed the House of Representatives and the Senate, shall, before it become a Law, be presented to the President of the United States; If he approve he shall sign it, but if not he shall return it, with his Objections to that House in which it shall have originated, who shall enter the Objections at large on their Journal, and proceed to reconsider it. If after such Reconsideration two thirds of that House shall agree to pass the Bill, it shall be sent, together with the Objections, to the other House, by which it shall likewise be reconsidered, and if approved by two thirds of that House, it shall become a Law. But in all such Cases the Votes of both Houses shall be determined by Yeas and Nays, and the Names of the Persons voting for and against the Bill shall be entered on the Journal of each House respectively. If any Bill shall not be returned by the President within ten Days (Sundays excepted) after it shall have been presented to him, the Same shall be a Law, in like Manner as if he had signed it, unless the Congress by their Adjournment prevent its Return, in which Case it shall not be a Law.

Every Order, Resolution, or Vote to which the Concurrence of the Senate and House of Representatives may be necessary (except on a question of Adjournment) shall be presented to the President of the United States; and before the Same shall take Effect, shall be approved by him, or being disapproved by him, shall be repassed by two thirds of the Senate and House of Representatives, according to the Rules and Limitations prescribed in the Case of a Bill.

Section 8 - Powers of Congress--The Congress shall have Power To lay and collect Taxes, Duties, Imposts and Excises, to pay the Debts and provide for the common Defence and general Welfare of the United States; but all Duties, Imposts and Excises shall be uniform throughout the United States;

To borrow money on the credit of the United States;

To regulate Commerce with foreign Nations, and among the several States, and with the Indian Tribes;

To establish an uniform Rule of Naturalization, and uniform Laws on the subject of Bankruptcies throughout the United States;

To coin Money, regulate the Value thereof, and of foreign Coin, and fix the Standard of Weights and Measures;

To provide for the Punishment of counterfeiting the Securities and current Coin of the United States;

To establish Post Offices and Post Roads;

To promote the Progress of Science and useful Arts, by securing for limited Times to Authors and Inventors the exclusive Right to their respective Writings and Discoveries;

To constitute Tribunals inferior to the supreme Court;

To define and punish Piracies and Felonies committed on the high Seas, and Offenses against the Law of Nations;

To declare War, grant Letters of Marque and Reprisal, and make Rules concerning Captures on Land and Water;

To raise and support Armies, but no Appropriation of Money to that Use shall be for a longer Term than two Years;

To provide and maintain a Navy;

To make Rules for the Government and Regulation of the land and naval Forces;

To provide for calling forth the Militia to execute the Laws of the Union, suppress Insurrections and repel Invasions;

To provide for organizing, arming, and disciplining the Militia, and for governing such Part of them as may be employed in the Service of the United States, reserving to the States respectively, the Appointment of the Officers, and the Authority of training the Militia according to the discipline prescribed by Congress;

To exercise exclusive Legislation in all Cases whatsoever, over such District (not exceeding ten Miles square) as may, by Cession of particular States, and the acceptance of Congress, become the Seat of the Government of the United States, and to exercise like Authority over all Places purchased by the Consent of the Legislature of the State in which the Same shall be, for the Erection of Forts, Magazines, Arsenals, dock-Yards, and other needful Buildings; And

To make all Laws which shall be necessary and proper for carrying into Execution the foregoing Powers, and all other Powers vested by this Constitution in the Government of the United States, or in any Department or Officer thereof.

Section 9 - Limits on Congress--The Migration or Importation of such Persons as any of the States now existing shall think proper to admit, shall not be prohibited by the Congress prior to the Year one thousand eight hundred and eight, but a tax or duty may be imposed on such Importation, not exceeding ten dollars for each Person.

The privilege of the Writ of Habeas Corpus shall not be suspended, unless when in Cases of Rebellion or Invasion the public Safety may require it.

No Bill of Attainder or ex post facto Law shall be passed.

(No capitation, or other direct, Tax shall be laid, unless in Proportion to the Census or Enumeration herein before directed to be taken.) **(Section in parentheses clarified by the 16th Amendment.)**

No Tax or Duty shall be laid on Articles exported from any State.

No Preference shall be given by any Regulation of Commerce or Revenue to the Ports of one State over those of another: nor shall Vessels bound to, or from, one State, be obliged to enter, clear, or pay Duties in another.

No Money shall be drawn from the Treasury, but in Consequence of Appropriations made by Law; and a regular Statement and Account of the Receipts and Expenditures of all public Money shall be published from time to time.

No Title of Nobility shall be granted by the United States: And no Person holding any Office of Profit or Trust under them, shall, without the Consent of the Congress, accept of any present, Emolument, Office, or Title, of any kind whatever, from any King, Prince or foreign State.

Section 10 - Powers prohibited of States

No State shall enter into any Treaty, Alliance, or Confederation; grant Letters of Marque and Reprisal; coin Money; emit Bills of Credit; make any Thing but gold and silver Coin a Tender in Payment of Debts; pass any Bill of Attainder, ex post facto Law, or Law impairing the Obligation of Contracts, or grant any Title of Nobility.

No State shall, without the Consent of the Congress, lay any Imposts or Duties on Imports or Exports, except what may be absolutely necessary for executing it's inspection Laws: and the net Produce of all Duties and Imposts, laid by any State on Imports or Exports, shall be for the Use of the Treasury of the United States; and all such Laws shall be subject to the Revision and Controul of the Congress.

No State shall, without the Consent of Congress, lay any duty of Tonnage, keep Troops, or Ships of War in time of Peace, enter into any Agreement or Compact with another State, or with a foreign Power, or engage in War, unless actually invaded, or in such imminent Danger as will not admit of delay.

Article II - The Executive Branch

Section 1 - The President The executive Power shall be vested in a President of the United States of America. He shall hold his Office during the Term of four Years, and, together with the Vice-President chosen for the same Term, be elected, as follows:

Each State shall appoint, in such Manner as the Legislature thereof may direct, a Number of Electors, equal to the whole Number of Senators and Representatives to which the State may be entitled in the Congress: but no Senator or Representative, or Person holding an Office of Trust or Profit under the United States, shall be appointed an Elector.

(The Electors shall meet in their respective States, and vote by Ballot for two persons, of whom one at least shall not lie an Inhabitant of the same

State with themselves. And they shall make a List of all the Persons voted for, and of the Number of Votes for each; which List they shall sign and certify, and transmit sealed to the Seat of the Government of the United States, directed to the President of the Senate. The President of the Senate shall, in the Presence of the Senate and House of Representatives, open all the Certificates, and the Votes shall then be counted. The Person having the greatest Number of Votes shall be the President, if such Number be a Majority of the whole Number of Electors appointed; and if there be more than one who have such Majority, and have an equal Number of Votes, then the House of Representatives shall immediately chuse by Ballot one of them for President; and if no Person have a Majority, then from the five highest on the List the said House shall in like Manner chuse the President. But in chusing the President, the Votes shall be taken by States, the Representation from each State having one Vote; a quorum for this Purpose shall consist of a Member or Members from two-thirds of the States, and a Majority of all the States shall be necessary to a Choice. In every Case, after the Choice of the President, the Person having the greatest Number of Votes of the Electors shall be the Vice President. But if there should remain two or more who have equal Votes, the Senate shall chuse from them by Ballot the Vice-President.) **(This clause in parentheses was superseded by the 12th Amendment.)**

The Congress may determine the Time of choosing the Electors, and the Day on which they shall give their Votes; which Day shall be the same throughout the United States.

No person except a natural born Citizen, or a Citizen of the United States, at the time of the Adoption of this Constitution, shall be eligible to the Office of President; neither shall any Person be eligible to that Office who shall not have attained to the Age of thirty-five Years, and been fourteen Years a Resident within the United States.

(In Case of the Removal of the President from Office, or of his Death, Resignation, or Inability to discharge the Powers and Duties of the said Office, the same shall devolve on the Vice President, and the Congress may by Law provide for the Case of Removal, Death, Resignation or Inability, both of the President and Vice President, declaring what Officer shall then act as President, and such Officer shall act accordingly, until the Disability be removed, or a President shall be elected.) **(This clause in parentheses has been modified by the 20th and 25th Amendments.)**

The President shall, at stated Times, receive for his Services, a Compensation, which shall neither be increased nor diminished during the Period for which he shall have been elected, and he shall not receive within that Period any other Emolument from the United States, or any of them.

Before he enter on the Execution of his Office, he shall take the following Oath or Affirmation:

"I do solemnly swear (or affirm) that I will faithfully execute the Office of President of the United States, and will to the best of my Ability, preserve, protect and defend the Constitution of the United States."

Section 2 - Civilian Power over Military, Cabinet, Pardon Power, Appointments--The President shall be Commander in Chief of the Army and Navy of the United States, and of the Militia of the several States, when called into the actual Service of the United States; he may require the Opinion, in writing, of the principal Officer in each of the executive Departments, upon any subject relating to the Duties of their respective Offices, and he shall have Power to Grant Reprieves and Pardons for Offenses against the United States, except in Cases of Impeachment.

He shall have Power, by and with the Advice and Consent of the Senate, to make Treaties, provided two thirds of the Senators present concur; and he shall nominate, and by and with the Advice and Consent of the Senate, shall appoint Ambassadors, other public Ministers and Consuls, Judges of the supreme Court, and all other Officers of the United States, whose Appointments are not herein otherwise provided for, and which shall be established by Law: but the Congress may by Law vest the Appointment of such inferior Officers, as they think proper, in the President alone, in the Courts of Law, or in the Heads of Departments.

The President shall have Power to fill up all Vacancies that may happen during the Recess of the Senate, by granting Commissions which shall expire at the End of their next Session.

Section 3 - State of the Union, Convening Congress--He shall from time to time give to the Congress Information of the State of the Union, and recommend to their Consideration such Measures as he shall judge necessary and expedient; he may, on extraordinary Occasions, convene both Houses, or either of them, and in Case of Disagreement between them, with Respect to the Time of Adjournment, he may adjourn them to such Time as he shall think proper; he shall receive Ambassadors and other public Ministers; he shall take Care that the Laws be faithfully executed, and shall Commission all the Officers of the United States.

Section 4 - Disqualification

The President, Vice President and all civil Officers of the United States, shall be removed from Office on Impeachment for, and Conviction of, Treason, Bribery, or other high Crimes and Misdemeanors.

Article III - The Judicial Branch

Section 1 - Judicial powers--The judicial Power of the United States, shall be vested in one supreme Court, and in such inferior Courts as the Congress may from time to time ordain and establish. The Judges, both of the supreme and inferior Courts, shall hold their Offices during good Behavior, and shall, at stated Times, receive for their Services a Compensation which shall not be diminished during their Continuance in Office.

Section 2 - Trial by Jury, Original Jurisdiction, Jury Trials--*(The judicial Power shall extend to all Cases, in Law and Equity, arising under this Constitution, the Laws of the United States, and Treaties made, or which shall be made, under their Authority; to all Cases affecting Ambassadors, other public Ministers and Consuls; to all Cases of admiralty and maritime Jurisdiction; to Controversies to which the United States shall be a Party; to Controversies between two or more States; between a State and Citizens of another State; between Citizens of different States; between Citizens of the same State claiming Lands under Grants of different States, and between a State, or the Citizens thereof, and foreign States, Citizens or Subjects.)* **(This section in parentheses is modified by the 11th Amendment.)**

In all Cases affecting Ambassadors, other public Ministers and Consuls, and those in which a State shall be Party, the supreme Court shall have original Jurisdiction. In all the other Cases before mentioned, the supreme Court shall have appellate Jurisdiction, both as to Law and Fact, with such Exceptions, and under such Regulations as the Congress shall make.

The Trial of all Crimes, except in Cases of Impeachment, shall be by Jury; and such Trial shall be held in the State where the said Crimes shall have been committed; but when not committed within any State, the Trial shall be at such Place or Places as the Congress may by Law have directed.

Section 3 - Treason *Note*--Treason against the United States, shall consist only in levying War against them, or in adhering to their Enemies, giving them Aid and Comfort. No Person shall be convicted of Treason unless on the Testimony of two Witnesses to the same overt Act, or on Confession in open Court.

The Congress shall have power to declare the Punishment of Treason, but no Attainder of Treason shall work Corruption of Blood, or Forfeiture except during the Life of the Person attainted.

Article IV - The States

Section 1 - Each State to Honor all others--Full Faith and Credit shall be given in each State to the public Acts, Records, and judicial Proceedings of every other State. And the Congress may by general Laws prescribe the Manner in which such Acts, Records and Proceedings shall be proved, and the Effect thereof.

Section 2 - State citizens, Extradition--The Citizens of each State shall be entitled to all Privileges and Immunities of Citizens in the several States.

A Person charged in any State with Treason, Felony, or other Crime, who shall flee from Justice, and be found in another State, shall on demand of the executive Authority of the State from which he fled, be delivered up, to be removed to the State having Jurisdiction of the Crime.

(No Person held to Service or Labour in one State, under the Laws thereof, escaping into another, shall, in Consequence of any Law or Regulation therein, be discharged from such Service or Labour, But shall be delivered up on Claim of the Party to whom such Service or Labour may be due.) **(This clause in parentheses is superseded by the 13th Amendment.)**

Section 3 - New States--New States may be admitted by the Congress into this Union; but no new States shall be formed or erected within the Jurisdiction of any other State; nor any State be formed by the Junction of two or more States, or parts of States, without the Consent of the Legislatures of the States concerned as well as of the Congress.

The Congress shall have Power to dispose of and make all needful Rules and Regulations respecting the Territory or other Property belonging to the United States; and nothing in this Constitution shall be so construed as to Prejudice any Claims of the United States, or of any particular State.

Section 4 - Republican government--The United States shall guarantee to every State in this Union a Republican Form of Government, and shall protect each of them against Invasion; and on Application of the Legislature, or of the Executive (when the Legislature cannot be convened) against domestic Violence.

The Ratification of the Conventions of nine States, shall be sufficient for the Establishment of this Constitution between the States so ratifying the Same.

Article V – Amendment

The Congress, whenever two thirds of both Houses shall deem it necessary, shall propose Amendments to this Constitution, or, on the Application of the Legislatures of two thirds of the several States, shall call a Convention for proposing Amendments, which, in either Case, shall be valid to all Intents and Purposes, as part of this Constitution, when ratified by the Legislatures of three fourths of the several States, or by Conventions in three fourths thereof, as the one or the other Mode of Ratification may be proposed by the Congress; Provided that no Amendment which may be made prior to the Year One thousand eight hundred and eight shall in any Manner affect the first and fourth Clauses in the Ninth Section of the first Article; and that no State, without its Consent, shall be deprived of its equal Suffrage in the Senate.

Article VI - Debts, Supremacy, Oaths

All Debts contracted and Engagements entered into, before the Adoption of this Constitution, shall be as valid against the United States under this Constitution, as under the Confederation.

This Constitution, and the Laws of the United States which shall be made in Pursuance thereof; and all Treaties made, or which shall be made, under the Authority of the United States, shall be the supreme Law of the Land; and the Judges in every State shall be bound thereby, any Thing in the Constitution or Laws of any State to the Contrary notwithstanding.

The Senators and Representatives before mentioned, and the Members of the several State Legislatures, and all executive and judicial Officers, both of the United States and of the several States, shall be bound by Oath or Affirmation, to support this Constitution; but no religious Test shall ever be required as a Qualification to any Office or public Trust under the United States.

Article VII – Ratification

The Ratification of the Conventions of nine States, shall be sufficient for the Establishment of this Constitution between the States so ratifying the Same. Done in Covvention by the Unanimous Consent of the States present the Seventeenth Day of September in the Year of our Lord one thousand seven hundred and Eighty seven and of the Independence on the United States of America the Twelfth In witness whereof We have hereunto subscribed our Names.

Bill of Rights
First ten Amendments to the Constitution

First Amendment addresses the rights of Freedom of religion (prohibiting Congressional establishment of a religion over another religion through Law and protecting the right to free exercise of religion), freedom of speech, freedom of the press, freedom of assembly, and freedom of petition.

Second Amendment: declares "a well regulated militia" as "necessary to the security of a free State", and as explanation for prohibiting infringement of "the right of the people to keep and bear arms"

Third Amendment: prohibits the government from using private homes as quarters for soldiers without the consent of the owners. The only existing case law regarding this amendment is a lower court decision in the case of Engblom v. *Carey*.

Fourth Amendment: guards against seizures of property without a specific warrant or a "probable cause" to believe a crime has been committed. Some rights to privacy have been inferred from this amendment and others by the Supreme Court.

Fifth Amendment: forbids trial for a major crime except after indictment by a grand jury; prohibits double jeopardy (repeated trials), except in certain very limited circumstances; forbids punishment without due process of law; and provides that an accused person may not be compelled to testify_against himself (this is also known as "Taking the Fifth" or "Pleading the Fifth"). This is regarded as the "rights of the accused" amendment, otherwise known as the Miranda rights after the Supreme Court case. It also prohibits government from taking private property without "just compensation," the basis of eminent domain in the United States.

Sixth Amendment: guarantees a speedy public trial for criminal offenses. It requires trial by a jury, guarantees the right to legal council for the accused, and guarantees that the accused may require witnesses to attend the trial and testify in the presence of the accused. It also guarantees the accused a right to know the charges against him. The Sixth Amendment has several court cases associated with it, including *Powell v. Alabama, United States v. Wong Kim Ark, Gideon v.*

Wainwright, and *Crawford v. Washington.* In 1966, the Supreme Court ruled that the Fifth Amendment prohibition on forced self-incrimination and the sixth amendment clause on right to counsel were to be made known to all persons placed under arrest, and these clauses have become known as the Miranda rights.

Seventh Amendment: assures trial by jury in civil cases.

Eighth Amendment: forbids excessive bail or fines, and cruel and unusual punishment.

Ninth Amendment: declares that the listing of individual rights in the Constitution and Bill of Rights is not meant to be comprehensive; and that the other rights not specifically mentioned are retained elsewhere by the people.

Tenth Amendment: provides that powers that the Constitution does not delegate to the United States and does not prohibit the States from exercising, are "reserved to the States respectively, or to the people."

Subsequent amendments (11–27)

Additional amendments to the United States Constitution

Eleventh Amendment (1795): Clarifies judicial power over foreign nationals, and limits ability of citizens to sue states in federal courts and under federal law.

Twelfth Amendment (1804): Changes the method of presidential elections so that members of the Electoral_College cast separate ballots for president and vice president.

Thirteenth Amendment (1865): Abolishes slavery and grants Congress power to enforce abolition.

Fourteenth Amendment (1868): Defines a set of guarantees for United States citizenship; prohibits *states* from abridging citizens' privileges or immunities and rights to due process and the equal protection of the law; repeals the Three-fifths compromise; prohibits repudiation of the federal debt caused by the Civil War.

Fifteenth Amendment (1870): Forbids the federal government and the states from using a citizen's race, color, or previous status as a slave as a qualification for voting.

Sixteenth Amend. (1913): Authorizes unapportioned federal taxes on income.

Seventeenth Amendment (1913): Establishes direct election of senators.

Eighteenth Amendment (1919): Prohibited the manufacturing, importing, and exporting of alcoholic beverages (see Prohibition in the United States). *Repealed by the Twenty-First Amendment.*

Nineteenth Amendment (1920): Prohibits the federal government and the states from forbidding any citizen to vote due to their sex.

Twentieth Amendment (1933): Changes details of Congressional and presidential terms and of presidential succession.

Twenty-first Amendment (1933): Repeals Eighteenth   Amendment. Permits states to prohibit the importation of alcoholic beverages.

Twenty-second Amendment (1951): Limits president to two terms

Twenty-Third Amendment (1961): Grants presidential electors to the District of Columbia

Twenty-fourth Amendment (1964): Prohibits the federal government and the states from requiring the payment of a tax as a qualification for voting for federal officials.)

Twenty-fifth Amendment (1967): Changes details of presidential succession, provides for temporary removal of president, and provides for replacement of the vice president.

Twenty-sixth Amendment (1971): Prohibits the federal government and the states from forbidding any citizen of age 18 or greater to vote simply because of their age.

Twenty-seventh Amend.. (1992): Limits congressional   pay raises.

Note: The full text of the amendments is not shown for clarity and simplification.

The Rise and Fall of the American Republic
(1787-1913) (1913-2009)

Benjamin Franklin, at the signing of the draft of the Constitution in 1787, commented on a painting near George Washington's chair. Franklin commented that it was always difficult for painters to show the difference between the rising sun and setting sun. He said that during the convention he had often looked at the painted sun and wondered "...whether it was rising or setting. But now at length I have the happiness to know that it is a rising and not a setting sun."

That painting symbolized the birth of a great nation. The great tragedy is that the same picture today could symbolize the death of a great nation. (Setting sun) The year 1913 was the beginning of the fall of our "Republic". In that year The Federal Reserve Act was passed allowing a private central bank to charge the American tax payer interest for loaning us our own money, the 16th Amendment was passed allowing the government to collect income taxes on peoples wages, and the 17th Amendment changed the way that state Senators were chosen reducing their ability to protect states' rights.

Prior to the 17th Amendment, the states could protect themselves from the Federal Government if the House tried to pass legislation against states' rights. The senators were appointed by the state legislature and could veto any legislation by the House that threatened states' rights. This amendment changed all that! Now the senators were to be elected by popular ballot rather than being appointed by the state legislature. Under this amendment the senators would be subjected to the same pressures as the members of the House. We may as well have 535 House members instead of 435 House members and 100 Senators.

These unjust amendments and the Federal Reserve Act passed in 1913 were, in effect, the beginning of the fall of our Republic. Now is the time to abolish the Federal Reserve Act and the 16th and 17th Amendments in order to return our country to that which was envisioned by our founding fathers. There is little time left if we are to accomplish this peaceably through the political process.

Together we can return our country to that which was envisioned by our founding fathers.

What do **true** Patriots stand for?

A government that:

- *Abides by the Constitution.*
- *Adopts sound monetary policies by abolishing the private* **Federal Reserve, Fractional Reserve Banking** *and* **Income Tax** *on our citizen's salaries.*
- *Stops trying to be the policeman of the world.*
- *Recognizes the sovereignty of the individual states and its citizens.*

Make your vote count. Vote for only those legislators that score 50% or higher on the Constitutional scorecard. Google (The Freedom Index) for a list of your representatives voting record.

Additional Publications by
J L Flinchpaugh Publishing Company
St. Joseph, Missouri
lflinch@stjoelive.com
www.larryflinchpaugh.com

Billion$ For The Banker$
Debts For The People

June 2009

$5.00

This 1984 informative reprint of Sheldon Emry's booklet will give the reader greater insight into our country's monetary system and explains why we must abolish the privately owned Federal Reserve Banking cartel that has, from 1913, been in charge of printing our money and loaning it to the American government with interest. The U.S. Treasury Department can print our money "Interest Free," making it unnecessary to pay income tax on our citizen's wages.

Sheldon Emry's original book was not copyrighted and neither is this one. The publisher, Larry Flinchpaugh, has added two extra sections to help bring the booklet up to date a bit. Even though some of the information is a little outdated it is still relevant today.

Contrary to popular belief, the only reason our paper money should be backed by gold and silver is because that is what is required by the Constitution. Paper money is only a means to account for the value a person adds to the economy through his labor, investment and risk. That plus the government's willingness to accept it as payment of taxes is the only backing it needs.

Consider purchasing several for your legislators and friends.

215

Growing Up In a Zoo

February 2011

$15.00

This is a story of Larry Flinchpaugh growing up in St. Joseph, Missouri in the 1940's through the 1960's and working in his parents Pet Shop, Zoo, and Reptile Gardens. The facility was located at 3727 Frederick Avenue-old highway 36. (Now the home of The Citizens Bank and Trust Company) The book is full of interesting and funny stories regarding his experience in training and handling their pet chimpanzee, Vicky Lynn. Vicky not only appeared regularly at the Krug Park Bowl, KFEQ TV, daily shows at the Zoo but even had a part in a Harvard Biology training film. Other stories include the part Larry played in the heroic Air Force flight from Homestead Air force base in Florida to Rosecrans Field in St. Joe. That flight saved the life of one of the Zoo's employees, Bill White, after he had been bitten by an Indian cobra. This story was carried by almost every major news outlet throughout the world.

There are many pictures and interesting stories included which should be of special interest to those who came from miles around to tour the facility and to be entertained and educated about a wide variety of animals, birds and reptiles. Even those people who never toured the Zoo but love animals and animal stories will find the stories entertaining and educational.

Vicky was one of the Flinchpaugh family Members. She ate with them in their private kitchen at the zoo facility but had her own sleeping cage. It was very sad when she reached the age of about eight and began to rebel.

Against All Odds
President Paul Ronan
$15.00

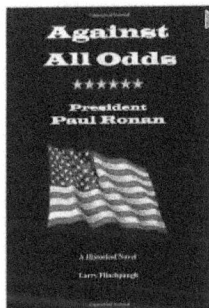

This exciting story follows the lives of four members of the Ronan family, from 1859-2012, as they influence the American political system to once again establish a Constitutional Republic.

In 1859, the protagonist, Sam Ronan comes to America from Ireland and becomes a telegraph operator in Philadelphia and shortly thereafter, he lands a job in *Breckenridge, Missouri* as a telegrapher for the *Hannibal and St. Joseph Railroad.*

Because the *Confederate bushwhackers* had sabotaged the bridge over the *Platt River*, Sam almost loses his life while traveling to St. Joe on the train. Having graduated from Harvard, magna cum laude, Sam's son Jeff lands a job working for President Woodrow Wilson in Washington, D.C.

Matt, Sam's grandson, meets the love of his life at the *Frog Hop Ball Room* in St. Joseph and becomes a successful farmer and Federal Congressman.

Graduating from *Central High School* in St. Joseph, Mo., Sam's great-grandson, Paul, obtains a medical degree from Baylor University in Texas and then joins the Navy and nearly loses his life when the Israelis attacked his reconnaissance ship, the *USS Liberty in 1967*. Honorably discharged from the Navy, Paul becomes a Texas Congressman and after a ruthless campaign in 2012, he is overwhelmingly *elected President of the United States*.

Each one of the four generations of the Ronan family added greatly to the security and financial wellbeing of this country's citizens. You will learn how Paul Ronan obtained full employment, truly "affordable" health care, a balanced budget, a plan to totally "pay off" the national debt, all in a candid *entertaining and educational story format.*

Letters Home From Civil War Soldier Charles W. Gamble

(1862-1864)

Compiled by Mark Flinchpaugh, April 2011.

$15.00

Mark Flinchpaugh's

Letters Home

From

Civil War Soldier

Charles Gamble

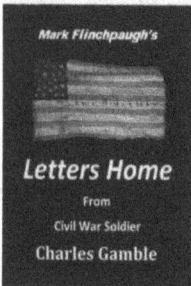

These historic letters included in this book were written in the 1860's by Union soldier, Charles W. Gamble, to his wife and family during the Civil War. He bravely served with the 12th regiment, New Jersey volunteers, Company D. A carpenter by trade, Charles joined the

Union Army in August, 1862 to, as he stated, "to preserve the country and the Constitution." *Note: Not to free the slaves.* Several times in his letters he frankly wrote that he might not come back home alive, but he was serving for a just cause. This is a fascinating and personal account of a common soldier's life serving his country and fighting to keep the Union intact. Told from the intimate perspective of a typical volunteer soldier, you will glean interesting tidbits of historical information not usually found in books about the Civil War.

You will come to feel that you know Charles personally as you read his actual letters about his daily activities during the war. From mundane chores to the horrors of battle at Gettysburg, you will experience Civil War life through Charles' own words.

No matter how difficult the hardships became Charles courageously pressed on for the good of the country. History comes alive in these insightful, heartwarming letters written nearly one hundred fifty years ago by Charles W. Gamble.

This book is available on Amazon.com and at all the St. Joseph libraries, book stores, most local museums and various tourist locations.

Should I Start My Own Business ?

January 20, 2013

$12.00

Should I Start My Own Business?

Accounting Reveals the Secrets of Failure of Your New Business

Sample Business Plan
Break Even Analysis
Accounting Terms Explained
Government Regulations
Much More

Larry Flinchpaugh

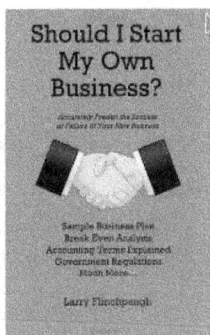

This self-help 127 page paperback book follows the various business ventures that Larry Flinchpaugh has been involved in from 1963 to 2005.

It starts out by asking the question, "Why do you want to start your own business?" Sadly many people start a business for the wrong reasons and many lose a good portion of their life savings in the first year or two.

This self-help 127 page paperback book follows the various business ventures that Larry Flinchpaugh has been involved in from 1963 to 2005.

It starts out by asking the question, "Why do you want to start your own business?" Sadly many people start a business for the wrong reasons and many lose a good portion of their life savings in the first year or two.

The book explains how to write a **"Business Plan"** and prepare a **"Break Even Analysis"** to help the reader predict their chance of success or failure.

Although, not intended to be an accounting book, it does explain basic accounting functions, how to calculate an individual's **"Net Worth"** and how to prepare a "Balance Sheet" and "Profit and Loss" statement.

This book is available at Hastings on the Belt Highway in St. Joseph, Missouri, Amazon.com/books and all St. Joseph, Missouri libraries. It can also be obtained at most local libraries thru their inter-library loan program.

Movie Documentary "This Is Our Town, St. Joseph, Missouri"
Filmed c. 1954 This movie was originally produced by "Robert M. Carson" productions on a 16MM film that was used as a promotional film for the city of St. Joe. It features several prominent businesses in St. Joe in the 1950's and shows nostalgic street scenes in a much different time.

The 16MM film was purchased by Mr. Flinchpaugh several years ago at a local estate sale from a former film collector. After retiring, Mr. Flinchpaugh re-discovered the long forgotten film in a box in his garage but noticed it had a strong odor smelling like bleach emitting from the metal film container. A quick check with "Accent Video" in Overland Park confirmed that the film was rapidly deteriorating and needed to be restored immediately before it was entirely lost.

The film has been shown several times at the local libraries and civic organizations but anyone wishing to purchase a copy of the film may buy one at "Hastings" most of the local museums, the "St. Joseph Visitor Center" and Hy-Vee on the Belt highway.

Specific viewings for local civic groups, churches, and other clubs and organization can still be arranged by calling Larry at 816-676-2565 or email him at lflinch@stjoelive.com.

Index